VCs of the North

VCs of the North

Cumbria, Durham and Northumberland

Alan Whitworth

Pen & Sword
MILITARY

First published in Great Britain in 2015 by
Pen & Sword Military
an imprint of
Pen & Sword Books Ltd
47 Church Street
Barnsley
South Yorkshire
S70 2AS

ISBN 978 1 47384 822 1

A CIP catalogue record for this book is available from the British
Library

Typeset in Ehrhardt by
Mac Style Ltd, Bridlington, East Yorkshire
Printed and bound in the UK by CPI Group (UK) Ltd,
Croydon, CRO 4YY

Pen & Sword Books Ltd incorporates the imprints of Pen & Sword
Archaeology, Atlas, Aviation, Battleground, Discovery, Family
History, History, Maritime, Military, Naval, Politics, Railways, Select,
Transport, True Crime, and Fiction, Frontline Books, Leo Cooper,
Praetorian Press, Seaforth Publishing and Wharncliffe.

For a complete list of Pen & Sword titles please contact
PEN & SWORD BOOKS LIMITED
47 Church Street, Barnsley, South Yorkshire, S70 2AS, England
E-mail: enquiries@pen-and-sword.co.uk
Website: www.pen-and-sword.co.uk

Contents

Acknowledgements

I should like to record here the generous assistance I have received from various people and organisations in the preparation of this book, in particular Roger Dowson, Beck Isle Museum, Pickering; Mr Brian Best, Victoria Cross Society, for his invaluable help; the Victoria Cross and George Cross Association; Rupert Harding and the staff of Pen & Sword for their guidance in bringing this work to fruition, in particular Jane Robson for her superb editing; and not least my wife Alma for her encouragement and patience while I ignored jobs about the house in order to undertake my research and writing.

Preface

It is now nearly 160 years since the instigation of the Victoria Cross by Royal Warrant dated 29 January 1856, 'the most democratic and at the same time the most exclusive of all' military honours awarded for courage in the face of the enemy, regardless of class, race or creed. The following year 1857 witnessed the first investiture of the Victoria Cross, when sixty-two men received their medals from HM Queen Victoria in Hyde Park on 26 June. Sailor Charles David Lucas, First Mate of HMS *Hecla*, was the very first Victoria Cross winner in the century and a half of its existence. Today there is as much interest in the deeds and men who carried them out as there was then when the *London Gazette* first began recording and publishing the Victoria Cross recipients within its pages.

The Victoria Cross was originally conceived as an award for all ranks of the Army and Navy who, in the presence of an enemy, had performed some signal act of valour or devotion to their country, but over time the conditions of award and scope for receipt have been extended to include virtually every citizen, including civilians and women. From its inception, the actual decoration was deliberately designed to be intrinsically 'worthless', simply a scrap of bronze without rich gems or precious metals. Its true worth lay in its associations, and it was an honour so rare that it was impossible to 'buy' or 'earn' it in the way several other high awards could be acquired. Though no specific comment on the medal's intrinsic lack of value was made in the inauguration warrant, this was the theory behind its creation, exemplified in spirit by a clause which stated that 'neither rank, nor long service, nor wounds, nor any other circumstances or condition whatsoever, save the merit of conspicuous bravery' should 'establish a sufficient claim to the honour'. This condition thereby placed 'all persons on a perfectly equal footing in relation to eligibility for the decoration' – the nearest thing to a completely democratic award ever created within the annals of military history. This aspect was further confirmed by the elective procedure laid down in those cases where a number of 'equally brave and distinguished persons' had been thought worthy of the honour. The names submitted to the sovereign were to be chosen by their fellow comrades in arms taking part in the action concerned.

Its recipients were to bear no special privilege of knighthood or companionship, banners or robes, and the award contains no ranks within itself. It is not an 'order of chivalry', such as the Order of the Garter or the Bath, as it was once erroneously described by King Edward VII – a point that its founder Queen Victoria was at pains to draw attention to; it was simply a decoration 'to be highly prized and eagerly sought after by the officers and men of our naval and military services'.

Pensions were granted to all holders of the Victoria Cross below commissioned rank. Initially a pension of £10 per year was made payable to all non-commissioned ranks. In July 1898 it was decided this amount might be increased in times of need, at discretion, to £50 and later to £75. It was not until 1959 that the pension was allowed irrespective of rank and increased to £100. In 1995 it was increased to £1,300, at which time there were thirty-three recipients still alive.

The 1856 warrant also provided for the expulsion of a holder if 'convicted of treason, Cowardice, Felony or for any infamous Crime, or if he be accused of any such offence and doth not after a reasonable time surrender himself to be tried for the same'. Liability to expulsion lasted for life, not just for a period of service, but the sovereign retained the right to restore the award. It has been forfeited on eight occasions.

The first man to forfeit the award was Edward St John Daniel, who took to drink and became dissolute. He was arrested on 21 June for sodomy with four subordinate officers. The Admiralty stated that he was 'accused of a disgraceful offence' and had deserted to evade inquiry. The alleged desertion appears to have been engineered by his captain and the Admiral of the Mediterranean Fleet to avoid unwelcome revelations at a court martial. Daniel fled to New Zealand, where he served with the Armed Constabulary Field Force; he died in 1868 during the Fenian disturbances among the Irish gold miners.

Others were erased from the register of holders after convictions ranging from theft of ten bushels of oats to bigamy. Colour Sergeant Edmund Fowler of the Royal Irish Regiment faced forfeiture after a conviction for embezzlement in 1887. He had been awarded his VC for his actions while serving as a private with the Cameroonians in March 1879, after storming and clearing a cave of armed Zulus who had just shot dead his officer. When the Secretary of State sought the Queen's permission to erase Fowler's name from the register, her secretary replied that she could not bring herself to approve it. Fowler had distinguished himself in earning the Cross and, as his sole punishment was a reduction to the ranks, it appeared that his offence could not have been so serious. 'He is still considered fit to serve the Queen, and Her Majesty thinks he should retain his VC' and so he did.

Those who forfeited the VC were also required to surrender the decoration itself. The Treasury Solicitor cautioned the War Office in 1908 that this was illegal, as the medal remained the property of the recipient. The War Office response was a catch-22 solution. It would return forfeited Crosses if the holders applied for them, but it would not inform them that they could do so: King George V ended the affair. His secretary wrote in 1920, 'The King feels so strongly that, no matter the crime … the decoration should not be forfeited. Even if a VC holder were to be sentenced to be hanged for murder, he should be allowed to wear the VC on the scaffold.'

This came much too late for Private Valentine Bambrick of the 60th Rifles. Having taken his discharge from the Army at Aldershot in 1863, he was celebrating his new freedom in a local public house when he discovered Commissariat Sergeant Russell hitting a woman in an upstairs room; Bambrick intervened and gave the sergeant a thorough beating. Russell brought a charge of assault against Bambrick and accused him of stealing his medals. The woman, the only witness, disappeared. Russell and his cronies testified convincingly, and Bambrick was sentenced to three years in Pentonville. Mortified by this injustice and by the erasure of his name from the VC register, Bambrick was found hanged in his cell on 1 April 1864, three months after his jailing. A note expressed his despair at the loss of his award. Private Bambrick was buried in an unmarked felon's grave.

There were no further erasures after 1908, and the names of the eight men who forfeited their awards have been restored to the register of holders. The present warrant still provides for the cancellation and annulment of an award holder and the removal of the recipient's name, but it seems unlikely that this will ever happen.

Exploitation of the Victoria Cross for gain, while technically not misconduct, was considered dishonourable, and remains virtually unheard of. Piper George Findlater of the Gordon Highlanders, was awarded his Victoria Cross for gallantry in the 1897 Tirah Campaign in India. Although shot in both feet during the charge on 20 October and in great pain, he sat erect under heavy fire and continued playing the regimental tune *Cock o' the North*. He was decorated by the Queen at Netley Hospital. His deed became renowned, and he was engaged to play the march on stage at London's Alhambra Theatre for £30 a week – an amount far in excess of his army pay. Some disapproving officers clubbed together to stop the performances, and General Sir Evelyn Wood, in full dress uniform, visited Dundas Slater, the theatre manager, and offered to pay Findlater's salary if the acts were cancelled. Slater laughingly refused, saying he had already spent £300 on advertising alone!

Since the original warrant, other warrants have been issued modifying or extending its provisions – in 1858, for instance, Queen Victoria decreed that the Cross could be won by those who 'may perform acts of conspicuous courage and bravery ... in circumstances of extreme danger, such as the occurrence of a fire on board ship, or of the floundering of a vessel at sea, or under any other circumstances in which ... life or public property may be saved'. In 1881, a new Victoria Cross warrant was signed which stated, 'Our Will and Pleasure is that the qualification (for the award of the Victoria Cross) shall be "conspicuous bravery or devotion to the country in the presence of the enemy"' – but for this stipulation, there would have been no need for the institution of the George Cross.

In 1902 HM King Edward VII approved the important principle of awarding it posthumously. In 1911 King George V admitted native officers and men of the Indian Army to eligibility and, in a lengthy warrant dated 22 May 1920, it was further extended to include the RAF, and 'matrons, sisters, nurses … serving regularly or temporarily under the orders, direction or supervision' of the military authorities, emphasising, however, that the VC 'shall only be awarded for most conspicuous bravery or some daring or pre-eminent act of valour or self-sacrifice or extreme devotion to duty in the presence of the enemy'.

Queen Victoria chose the design for the new decoration herself, a cross patée in bronze, bearing the royal crest in its centre surmounting a scroll bearing the inscription *For Valour*. It is connected by a V-shaped link to a bar engraved on the face with laurel leaves, and having a space on the reverse for the recipient's name. The date of the deed for which the honour is bestowed is engraved on the back of the Cross itself. It is worn on the left breast suspended from a 1½-inch wide ribbon. Initially, the Cross was suspended on a royal blue ribbon for naval personnel, and a red ribbon for army recipients; but in the royal warrant dated 22 May 1920 it was decreed that henceforth all Victoria Crosses would be hung from a plain crimson ribbon, irrespective of the recipient's parent service.

The actual Cross in size measures little more than an inch square (35mm) and weighs nearly one ounce (27grams[1]), calculated from the fact that 12 finished medals together weigh 10–11 ounces,[2] and is cast in bronze from metal melted down from the cascabels (a large knob at the rear of the cannon on to which ropes were tied in order to man-handle the gun) of cannons captured from the Russians at Sebastopol in the Crimean War, and fashioned by the London firm of Messrs Hancock, who made the very first Victoria Cross and have continued to do so: the last remaining cascabel is tended by 15 Regiment Royal Logistic Corps at Donnington. Because they are cast and chased, no two Victoria Cross medals are exactly alike, and it seems fitting that each uniquely gallant act should be honoured by a decoration that itself remains unique.

Although the royal warrant instituting the Victoria Cross was not issued until January 1856, the earliest deed of valour to win the award was performed nineteen months earlier, on 21 June 1854, by a 20-year-old Irishman, Charles Davis Lucas, Mate of *HMS Hecla* which was attacking the fortress of Bomarsund in the Baltic. At a range of only 500 yards a live shell with fuse still hissing landed on the deck of the *Hecla*, from a Russian battery. Lucas picked it up with his bare hands and threw it overboard – it exploded as it entered the sea, but the ship and crew were saved from certain destruction. Lucas was promoted to Lieutenant on the spot by his commanding officer and eventually rose to the rank of Rear-Admiral. An interesting aside to this was that the very first Victoria Cross awarded was actually lost, along with other medals, on a railway journey and never recovered and a replacement had to be made which was never inscribed.

Some sixty-two VCs who had been 'gazetted' – i.e. their names and deeds cited in the *London Gazette* (which still takes place) – were present at Hyde Park, London, on the morning of 26 June 1857, when Queen Victoria held her first investiture ceremony for the newly instituted decoration that bore her name. In keeping with the democratic spirit of the award all recipients stood shoulder to shoulder, regardless of rank, while Her Majesty actually presented the decoration to each man from horseback.

Today the Victoria Cross remains the supreme British award, taking absolute precedence over all other awards and decorations. In the 150 years of its existence, there have been 1,357 awards.[3] Of these, 633 were won in the 1914–18 war, and 182 in the 1939–45 war. These totals include three awards of a Bar to the VC – in effect, 'double VCs'. At the time of writing just thirteen holders of the Victoria Cross are still alive, including one 'Northern' recipient.

Since the end of the Second World War the original VC has been awarded only fifteen times, four in the Korean War, one in the Indonesia-Malaysia confrontation in 1965, four to Australians in the Vietnam War, two during the Falkland's War in 1982, one in the Iraq War in 2004, and three in the war in Afghanistan in 2006 and 2012, the latter being awarded posthumously to L/Cpl James Ashworth: the last living person to receive the VC was L/Cpl Johnson Beharry of the 1st Battalion, the Princess of Wales's Royal Regiment while serving in Iraq in 2004.[4]

Among that roll of brave, within these pages the reader will find listed briefly the names, dates and deeds of just under fifty men from the northern counties of Cumbria, Durham and Northumberland who have been awarded the Victoria Cross medal. These men were either born and bred, or lived and died in these counties, or played a significant role in northern life, as in the instance of the Honourable Henry Hugh Manvers Percy, later knighted to become Lord Percy, who was Member of Parliament for North Northumberland 1865–8 and whose family seat is Alnwick Castle. As a body they make up almost one-tenth of the total of Victoria Cross recipients, and indeed, if we included VC holders who served in northern regiments, but who were not born or did not live in these counties, undoubtedly the percentage would be well over 10 per cent of the total. However, by choice, my decision is only to include those with significant personal northern connections rather than regimental connections.

Within this group of northern VC recipients are a number of 'firsts' to hold our interest, for instance, it was 2nd/Lt. Richard Annand who gained the first VC of the Second World War. Lieutenant-Colonel Roland Bradford, was one of only four sets of brothers to have secured the VC. He and his brother George were the only brothers to win a VC in the First World War and the last of the four sets to win the Victoria Cross. Roland Bradford also had the distinction of being the youngest General in the British Army. Then there is the youngest Victoria Cross recipient who won his award aged just 19.

Finally, it might be interesting to conclude with a few words about an aspect of the Victoria Cross not usually mentioned. Since 1879 more than 300 VC medals have been publicly auctioned or advertised for sale. Others have been privately sold. The monetary value of the VC can be seen in the increasing sums that the medals reach at auction. In 1955 the set of medals awarded to Edmund B Hartley were bought at Sotherby's for the then record price of £300. In October 1966 the Middlesex Regiment paid a new record figure of £900 for a Victoria Cross awarded after the Battle of the Somme. In January 1969 the record reached £1,700 for the medal set of William Rennie. In April 2004 the VC awarded to Sergeant Jackson, RAF, was sold at auction for £235,250. On 24 July 2006 an auction at Bonham's in Sydney, Australia, of the VC awarded to Captain Alfred Shout fetched a world-record hammer price of A$1million (approximately £410,000 at the then current exchange rate).

Alan Whitworth
Whitby, December 2014

Notes

1. Information supplied by Brian Best, Victoria Cross Society.
2. John Glanfield, *Bravest of the Brave: The Story of the Victoria Cross* (Sutton Publishing, 2005).
3. This figure is made up of the following: 1,353 individuals; 3 double VCs; 1 to an unknown American soldier.
4. On 26 Feb. 2015 the VC was awarded to L/Cpl Joshua Leakey, Parachute Regiment for his actions in Afghanistan. He is the third serviceman – and the first living serviceman – to receive the award for service in this country.

British Army Campaigns 1660–2000

Dates	War	Campaigns	Medals Awarded
1660–84	Against the Moors	Tangier	
1685	Monmouth Rebellion		
1689	Scottish		
1689–91	Against James II	Ireland	
1690–7	War of the Grand Alliance	Low Countries	
1701–13	War of Spanish Succession	Low Countries	
		Spain	
1715	Against the Old Pretender	Scotland	
1739–42	War of Jenkins' Ear	South America	
1741–8	War of Austrian Succession	Flanders	
		Germany	
		India	
		North America	
1745–6	Against the Young Pretender	England	
		Scotland	
1756–63	Seven Years War	Germany	
		Canada	
		West Indies	
		India	
		Mediterranean	

Date	Campaign	Theatre	Medal
1771–1819	Maharatta Wars	India	1st India Medal (17 bars)
1793–1815	Napoleonic Wars	West Indies	Gold Medals & West Indies Cross (officers only)
		Gibraltar	
		India	Seringapatam Medal
		Low Countries	
		Mediterranean	Military GSM
		Egypt	(GSM 23 bars, sanctioned 1847)
		South America	
		Portugal–Spain	
		India	
		South Africa	
		Waterloo	Waterloo Medal
1812–14	American War	North America	Military GSM (3 bars)
1814–16	Nepalese War	India	1st India Medal (bar)
1824–6	First Burma War		1st Burma Medal
1824–31	Ashanti War	West Africa	
1834–5	Kaffir War	South Africa	Medal for S Africa
1839–42	First Afghan War		Medal for Capture of Guznee
			Jellalabad Medal
			Candahar, Guhznee & Cabu Medal
			Medal for Defence of Kelat-I-Ghilzie
1841–2	First China War	China	China Medal
1843	Subjugation of Sinde	India	Sinde Medal
1843	Gwalior Campaign	India	Star for Gwalior Campaign
1845–6	First Sikh War	India	Medal for Sutlej Campaign (4 bars)
1845–7	First Maori War	New Zealand	New Zealand Medal
1846–7	Kaffir War	South Africa	Medal for S Africa
1848–9	Second Sikh War	India	Punjab Medal (3 bars)
1850–3	Kaffir War	South Africa	Medal for S Africa
1852	2nd Burmese War	India	India GSM (1854) (1 bar)
1854–6	Crimean War	Crimea	Crimea Medal (4 bars)
1856–7	Persian War	India	India GSM (1854) (1 bar)
1857–8	Indian Mutiny	India	Indian Mutiny Medal (5 bars)

Dates	War	Campaigns	Medals Awarded
1857–60	Second China War	China Medal	
1860–70	2nd/3rd Maori Wars	New Zealand Medal	
1863	Umbeyla Expedition	India	India GSM (1854) (1 bar
1866	Fenian Raid	Canada	GSM (1899) (1 bar)
1867–8	Abyssinian Expedition	Abyssinian Medal	
1873–4	Ashanti War	West Africa	Ashanti Medal
1870	Red River	Canada	GSM (1899) (2 bars)
1878–80	2nd Afghan War	Medal for Afghanistan (6 bars)	
	Kabul to Kandahar Star		
1870–80	Minor Expeditions	Bhutan	Each a Bar to India GSM (1854)
		Looshai	
		Jowaki	
		Nagaland	
1877–9	Zulu War	South Africa	Medal for S Africa (6 bars)
1880–1	Basutoland/Transkei	Cape of Good Hope	GSM (2 bars)
1881	First Boer War		
1882	Egyptian Campaign		Egyptian Medal (2 bars)
			Khedive's Star
1844–89	Sudan Campaign		Egyptian Medal (11 bars)
1885	Van Riel's Rebellion	Canada	North-West Canada Medal (1 bar)
1885–7	2nd Burmese War	India	India GSM (1854) (1 bar)
1888	Sikkim Campaign	Burma 1887–9	India GSM (1854) (1 bar)
1882–92	Operations NE Frontier of India and Burma	Hazara 1888	Each a bar to India GSM
		Chin-Lushai	(1854)
		Burma 1889–90	
		Burma 1889–92	

Date	Campaign	Place	Medal
		Samana 1891	
		Hazara 1891	
		Hunza 1891	
		NE Frontier 1891	
		Chin Hills 1892–3	
		Kachin Hills 1892–3	
1891–8	Central Africa		Central Africa Medal (1 bar)
1893	Matabele War	East Africa	Chartered Co. of S Africa Medal (2 bars)
1894–5	Waziristan Campaign	India	India GSM (1854) (1 bar)
1895	Chitral Campaign	India	India GSM (1854) (2 bars)
1895–6	3rd Ashanti War	West Africa	Ashanti Star
1896–7	Rhodesia		Chartered Co. of S Africa Medal (2 bars)
1896–7	Expeditions	West Africa	Royal Niger Company's in Nigeria Medal (1 bar)
1896–8	Sudan		Sudan Medal
1897–8	Indian Frontier Expeditions	Malakand 1897 Samana 1897 Punjab 1897 Frontier 1897–8 Tirah 1897–8	Each a bar to India Medal (1895)
1897–8	Operations in Uganda and Somaliland		East & Central Africa Medal (3 bars)
1899–1902	Second Boer War	South Africa	S Africa Medal (Queen's) (28 bars) King Edward's S Africa Medal (2 bars)
1900	Boxer Rebellion	China	China Medal (3 bars)
1900–20	Numerous small expeditions in East and West Africa	Africa	GSM (1902) (43 bars)
1901	Ashanti Rebellion	West Africa	Ashanti Medal (1 bar)
1901–2	Waziristan	India	India Medal (1895) (1 bar)
1903–4	Tibetan Expedition		Tibet Medal (1 bar)
1906	Zulu Rising	South Africa	Medal for Zulu Rising in Natal (1 bar)
1908	NW Frontier of India		India GSM (1908) (1 bar)
1911–12	Abor Expedition	NE Frontier of India	India GSM (1908) (1 bar)

Dates	War	Campaigns	Medals Awarded
1914–18	**First World War**	France/Flanders	1914 Star
		SW Africa	1914–15 Star
		SE Africa	British War Medal
		China	Victory Medal
		Dardanelles	
		Egypt	
		Palestine	
		Mesopotamia	
		Salonika	
		Italy	
		Russia	
		NW Frontier India	
1919	3rd Afghan War		India GSM (1908) (1 bar)
1919–20	Russia		
1919–20	Mahsud Expedition		India GSM (1908) (1 bar)
1919–21	Arab Insurrection	Mesopotamia	GSM (1919) (5 bars)
1919–21	Ireland		
1919–21	Waziristan		India GSM (1908) (1 bar)
1921–2	Malabar Rebellion		India GSM (1908) (1 bar)
1930–1	Waziristan		India GSM (1908) (1 bar)
1930–2	Burma		India GSM (1908) (1 bar)
1933	Mohmand Expedition		India GSM (1908) (1 bar)
1935	NW Frontier of India		India GSM (1908) (1 bar)
1936–39	Arab Rebellion		Palestine GSM (1918) (1 bar)
1936–9	NW Frontier of India		India GSM (1936) (2 bars)
1939–45	**Second World War**	Norway	1939–45 Star
		France	Africa Star
		Flanders 1939–40	Italy Star

Date	Campaign		Medal
	East Africa 1940–1		Pacific Star
	North Africa 1940–3		Burma Star
	Greece/Crete 1941		France & Germany Star
	Hong Kong 1941		Atlantic Star
	Iraq/Syria 1941		Defence Medal
	Malaya/Singapore 1941–2		Victory Medal
	Burma 1942–5		
	Sicily/Italy 1943–5		
	NW Europe 1944–5		
1945–6	SE Asia		GSM (1918) (1 bar)
		Indo-China	
		Dutch East Indies	
1945–8	Palestine		GSM (1918) (1 bar)
1948–60	Malaya		GSM (1918) (1 bar)
1950–3	Korean War		Korean Medal, UN Service Medal
1952–6	Mau Mau Rebellion	Kenya	Africa GSM (1 bar)
1954–60	Cyprus		GSM (1918) (1 bar)
1956	Suez Expedition		GSM (1918) (1 bar)
1957–9	Muscat and Oman		GSM (1918) (1 bar)
1962	Brunei Revolt		GSM (1918) (1 bar)
1963–6	Borneo Campaign		GSM (1962) (3 bars)
1964–	Cyprus, UN Peacekeeping Duty		UN Peacekeeping Medal
1964–7	Aden/Radfan		GSM (1962) (2 bars)
1969–2007	Northern Ireland		GSM (1962) (1 bar)
1979	Zimbabwe		Zimbabwe Medal
1982	Falklands Campaign		South Atlantic Medal
1983–4	Lebanon, Multinational Force		GSM (1962) (1 bar)
1991	Gulf War		Gulf War Medal
1992–5	Bosnia & Herzegovina		UN & NATO Medal
1994	Rwanda		UN Medal
1999	Sierra Leone		UN Medal
2001–14	Afghanistan		UN Medal

Cumbria Victoria Cross Holders

ACTON, Abraham
Rank/Service: Private, 2nd Bn King's Own (Royal) Border Regiment
VC Location: The Beacon, Whitehaven, Cumbria
Date of Gazette: 18 February 1915
Place/Date of Birth: Whitehaven, Cumbria, 17 December 1892
Place/Date of Death: Festubert, France, 19 May 1915
Grave: Commemorated on the Le Touret Memorial to the Missing (Panel 19-20), Le Touret Military Cemetery, Richebourg-l'Avoue, Pas de Calais, France
Town/County Connections: Whitehaven

Account of Deed: On 21 December, at Rouges-Bancs, France, both Acton and James Alexander Smith VC voluntarily left their trench and rescued a wounded man who had been lying exposed against the enemy's trenches for fifteen hours; and on the same day again left a British trench voluntarily, under heavy fire, to bring into cover another wounded man. He was under fire for sixty minutes whilst conveying the wounded men into safety.

Biographical Detail: 'Abe' Acton was born on 17 December 1893 to Robert and Elizabeth Eleanor Acton, of 4 Regent Square, Senhouse Street, Whitehaven, Cumbria. Abraham aged 22 and his brother Robert enlisted with the Territorial Army and served with A Company 5th Battalion Border Regiment. Upon the recommendation of Whitehaven Colliery Company manager, Robert Blair, who was an officer in the Territorial Army, Acton became a regular soldier, in January 1914. After war was declared, the following August, he was posted to France, along with many other West Cumbrian soldiers including Pte James Smith VC on 25 November 1914.

Later his VC deed was recounted in an advert for Zam Buk Ointment on the back cover of *The Illustrated London News* of 17 April 1915.

Of the two men who were rescued in this action, one was from Whitehaven and one from the Carlisle area. The Whitehaven soldier was Pte David ('Jimmy') Ross, whose family at one time lived at Rosemary Lane, Whitehaven, and like Abraham, had also attended Hogarth Mission.

Unfortunately, before the medal could be awarded he was killed in action at Festubert on 19 May 1915 and his body was never found – Acton is commemorated on the Le Touret Memorial. A service in his memory was held at Hogarth Mission on 6 June 1915. His VC medal was presented to his parents by HM King George V at Buckingham Palace on 29 November 1916.

After the war, Robert and Elizabeth Acton moved to Douglas, Isle of Man, where two of their married daughters lived and Abraham is commemorated on St Matthew's church War Memorial, Douglas. Pte Acton's medal was donated to the Whitehaven museum many years ago by his youngest brother, Charles Acton.

The Whitehaven museum collection kept at The Beacon holds a portrait of Abraham Acton. It was presented by the noted local artist J D Kenworthy to Whitehaven Borough Council. There is also a brass plaque that had been erected at Crosthwaite School in Rosemary Lane where he had been educated. A plaque marks his birthplace in Roper Street (Tyson's Court). He is named on the War Memorial in the church of St James, Whitehaven. He is named on a memorial bench, Orange Order, Helens Tower, Thiepval, France and also on the Regimental VC Memorial, Carlisle Cathedral.

Robert Acton, Abraham Acton's father, passed away on 10 January 1940, and Elizabeth Acton, his mother, on 5 November 1944. Abraham Acton's youngest brother, Harold Acton, died at the age of 93 in June 2006.

CHRISTIAN, Harry
Rank / Service: Private (later Cpl), 2nd Bn King's Own (Royal) Lancaster Regiment
VC Location: King's Own Royal Regiment Museum, Lancaster
Date of Gazette: 3 March 1916
Place / Date of Birth: Pennington, Cumbria, 17 January 1891
Place / Date of Death: West Cumberland Hospital, Whitehaven, 2 September 1974
Grave: Egremont Cemetery
Town / County Connections: Pennington; Whitehaven

Account of Deed: Private Christian was holding a crater with five or six men in front of British trenches at Cuinchy, France on 18 October 1915. The enemy commenced a very heavy bombardment of the position with heavy 'minenwerfer' bombs, forcing a temporary withdrawal. When he found that three men were missing, Private Christian at once returned alone to the crater, and, although bombs were continually bursting actually on the edge of the crater, he found, dug out, and carried one by one into safety all three men, thereby undoubtedly saving their lives. Later he placed himself where he could see the bombs coming, and directed his comrades when and where to seek cover.

Biographical Detail: Born in 1891 at Wallthwaite, Pennington, near Ulverston, Harry Christian was educated at the National School in Ulverston. After several farming jobs he enlisted in the King's Own in 1910 and was posted to the 2nd Battalion in India. Having returned to England with his unit in December 1914, he was sent to France in February 1915.

Badly wounded Christian was returned home. In September 1917 he received his Victoria Cross from King George V in Glasgow. This was the first Victoria Cross to be awarded to the Regiment in the war. He later returned to the 2nd Battalion in Salonika and was eventually discharged in 1919. For forty years he was landlord at the Park Head Inn, Egremont, Cumbria, and was a lifelong member of the Regimental Association. He died at Thornhill, Egremont, on 2 September 1974, aged 82.

His Victoria Cross and other medals were purchased in 1974 by the King's Own Royal Regiment Museum.

FORSHAW, William Thomas
Rank/Service: Lieutenant, 9th Manchester Regiment Territorials
VC Location: Manchester Regiment Museum, Ashton Town Hall
Date of Gazette: 17 June 1879
Place/Date of Birth: Barrow-in-Furness, Cumbria, 20 April 1890
Place/Date of Death: Maidenhead, Kent, 26 May 1943
Grave: Touchen End churchyard, near Bray, Berkshire
Memorials: In 1966 a Blue Plaque was placed at Ladysmith Barracks, Ashton-under-Lyne to honour his memory
Town/County Connections: Barrow-in-Furness, Cumbria; Ashton-under-Lyne; Ipswich; Maidenhead, Berkshire

Account of Deed: At Suvla Bay, Gallipoli, from 7 to 9 August 1915 Lieutenant Forshaw was attacked and heavily bombed by Turkish forces, repeatedly advancing through trenches and continually driven back by Forshaw, who directed and encouraged his men, exposing himself with the utmost disregard to danger, casually lighting bomb fuses with his cigarette, and throwing them at the enemy lines for forty-one hours. This action also earned him the nickname 'the Cigarette VC'. Later, during the night of 8/9 August he led his men forward, armed only with his revolver, and recaptured the trenches which had been taken.

Biographical Detail: William Thomas Forshaw was born in Barrow-in-Furness in Cumbria on 20 April 1890, the son of Thomas and Elizabeth. William was their eldest child; he had a younger brother named Frank. Thomas worked as a pattern maker and foreman at the shipbuilding firm Vickers, based in the town. William grew up at 105 Scott Street and attended Holker Street Boys School and Barrow Municipal Secondary School. He then went to Westminster College in London for two years.

William trained as a schoolteacher, and began his career in January 1912 at Dallas Road Council School and Sulyard Street Council School in Lancaster. The next year he moved to Manchester to work at North Manchester School in Higher Broughton.

Later in 1913 William joined the Ashton-under-Lyne Operatic Society. He performed in their production of *The Duchess of Dantzic*, by Ivan Caryll and Henry Hamilton, at the town's Hippodrome Theatre during February 1914.

In March William was commissioned as a 2nd Lieutenant in the 9th Battalion of the Manchester Regiment. This was a unit of the Territorial Force based in Ashton. Some of William's friends in the Operatic Society were also members of the battalion. This was a part-time commission.

At the outbreak of the First World War Forshaw volunteered to serve overseas in the 9th Battalion Manchester Regiment Territorials and by May 1915 he was serving in the Dardanelles where he won his VC at Suvla Bay, Gallipoli.

Taken ill, William was evacuated back to England. By 12 October he had returned to his parents' home in Ulverston, Cumbria, on sick leave. As news of his VC spread he became a well-known figure and he gave several newspaper interviews. On 16 October he paid a quiet visit to Ashton-under-Lyne, but it had to be cut short when he was ordered to London to receive his Victoria Cross.

William took Thomas and Frank to Buckingham Palace on 18 October, where he was invested with his VC by King George V.

Towards the end of that month William visited Barrow and Ashton. In Barrow on 27 October he was greeted by tens of thousands of people as he paraded through the town. He was then presented with a specially engraved sword by the town council. William also visited his old school, where he presented sports prizes and was able to convince the governors to give the pupils an extra day's holiday. William visited Ashton on the 30th. Again thousands of people filled the streets to greet him. He was granted the Freedom of the Borough by the Mayor of Ashton at a special Council Meeting.

On 2 November William was promoted to Captain, and he returned to duty. He spent much of 1916 and 1917 touring the country in attempts to raise civilian morale.

William married Sadie Mollie Lee-Heppel on 5 February 1916 in Barnet Registry Office, north London. She was a nurse at a military hospital in Caterham, Surrey, where William had occasionally been treated. William lived on Nether Street in North Finchley, London, at this time.

In October 1917 William left for India on active service. He was attached to the 76th Punjabis on 17 October. By October 1918 he was assigned to the 1st Battalion where he held the rank of Lieutenant.

William commanded a company in the 1st Battalion, and served with them until May 1919 when he became Staff Captain to the Poona Brigade, later holding this job in the 67th Brigade. He took part in the defeat of tribal rebellions in Waziristan, part of modern Pakistan, between 1919 and 1921. He was mentioned in despatches for this service; this qualified him to receive the 'Mahsud 1919–20' and 'Waziristan 1919–21' clasps.

During 1921 William attended a course at the British Army School of Education at Wellington in the Nilgiri Mountains of southern India. Whilst there he was attached to the 1st Battalion of the Suffolk Regiment as they fought the Malabar Rebellion; he received the 'Malabar 1921–2' clasp for this service.

William spent the rest of 1921 as the General Staff Officer Grade 3 responsible for Education at Southern Command. After this post was abolished he spent some time attached to the 1st Indian Infantry Group before retiring from the Army on 3 November 1922.

Forshaw attempted to return to teaching. He struggled to find work in England and eventually worked for two years in Egypt for the Royal Air Force Education Service. Returning home he and Sadie moved to Ipswich, where William went to work at Ipswich Central School. He later tried, unsuccessfully, to establish his own preparatory school, unfortunately the failure bankrupted him in 1929. William later worked for Gaumont British filmmakers, in their industrial film department.

On 9 November 1929 William was presented with a 'duplicate Victoria Cross' by Hancock's jewellers, the manufacturer; it is not known what had happened to his original medal. On the same day he attended the

VC Dinner in the House of Lords, along with eight other Manchester Regiment holders of the medal.

As the Second World War broke out in September 1939, William was too old to rejoin the Army, so he served in the 11th City of London (Dagenham) Home Guard as a Major. He commanded units based at the Murex Ironworks and anti-aircraft guns in Barking Park.

William and Sadie lived on Woodlands Road near Hornchurch in Essex during the early part of the war. During 1943 they moved to Foxearth Cottage in Holyport near Maidenhead, Berkshire. They had not been there long when William collapsed and died of a heart attack on 26 May. He was 53 years old.

Sadie died in early 1952 aged 72. They had no children, and William's grave had no headstone, so for many years its location was unknown, but in 1994 after strenuous research it was discovered that he was buried in Touchen End churchyard, near Bray in Berkshire.

William's Victoria Cross was put up for auction in 1964 where it was bought by the 9th Battalion of the Manchester Regiment and it is on display in the Museum of the Manchester Regiment in Ashton Town Hall in a gallery that is named after him. Interestingly, the sword he was presented with in Ashton-under-Lyne was discovered being used as a prop in the drama department of a local school at Ashton. Its importance was only realised when someone read the dedicatory inscription on the blade. This too, along with a silver tea service presented by North Manchester High School for Boys in Mosten, where he taught English for some years before the war, is also in the regimental museum.

HEWITSON, James

Rank/Service: Corporal, 4th Bn King's Own (Royal) Lancaster Regiment
VC Location: Privately held
Date of Gazette: 28 June 1918
Place/Date of Birth: Coniston, 15 October 1892
Place/Date of Death: Ulverston, Cumbria, 2 March 1963
Grave: St Andrew's churchyard, Coniston
Town/County Connections: Coniston; Ulverston, Cumbria

Account of Deed: Lance-Corporal Hewitson won his Victoria Cross near Givenchy on 26 April 1918.

For most conspicuous bravery, initiative and daring action. In a daylight attack on a series of crater posts L/Cpl Hewitson led his party to their objective with dash and vigour, clearing the enemy from both trench and dugouts, killing in one dugout six of the enemy who would not surrender. After capturing the final objective, he observed a hostile machine-gun team coming into action against his men. Working his way round the edge of the crater he attacked the team, killing four and capturing one. Shortly afterwards he engaged a hostile bombing party which was attacking a Lewis gun post; he routed the party, killing six of them. The extraordinary feats of daring performed by this gallant non-commissioned officer crushed the hostile opposition at this point.

Biographical Detail: James Hewitson was born at Thwaite Farm, Coniston, on 5 October 1892. Educated at Coniston CE School, he enlisted in the 8th (Service) Battalion King's Own on 17 November 1914 and later transferred to the 1/4th Battalion (Territorial Force). He was recommended on 8 May 1918 for the award, which was published in the *London Gazette* of 28 June 1918.

Promoted to Corporal, Hewitson received his VC from King George V in France on 8 August 1918 and returned home to a civic welcome in Coniston. Until his death, on 2 March 1963, James Hewitson lived and worked in Coniston and is buried in the parish churchyard.

JEFFERSON, Francis Arthur
Rank/Service: Lance-Corporal, 2nd Bn Lancashire Fusiliers
VC Location: Unknown
Date of Gazette: 13 July 1944
Place/Date of Birth: Ulverston, Cumbria, 18 August 1921
Place/Date of Death: Bolton, Lancashire, 4 September 1982
Grave:
Town/County Connections: Ulverston, Cumbria

Account of Deed: On 16 May 1944, during an attack on the Gustav Line, Monte Cassino, Italy, the leading company of Fusilier Jefferson's battalion had to dig in without protection. The enemy counter-attacked opening fire at short range, and Fusilier Jefferson on his own initiative seized a PIAT gun and, running forward under a hail of bullets, fired on the leading tank. It burst into flames and its crew were killed. The fusilier then reloaded and went towards the second tank which withdrew before he could get within range. By this time, British tanks had arrived and the enemy counter-attack was smashed.

Soon after his action, Jefferson left an account of his deeds in his own words.

I joined the army in 1942 and went to Africa in May 1943 with reinforcements for the Lancashire Fusiliers. I arrived too late for the African campaign and the first real action I saw was in Sicily with the Eighth Army. Soon after that we really got down to business, after landing at Taranto on the Adriatic coast of Italy. I was in Italy for the next eleven months during which time I took part in the fighting at Termoli, the Sangro crossing and the famous battle of Monastery Hill [Monte Cassino].

After a short rest period our division was brought in for the big push against the Gustav Line. During the first attack our Company's objective was two small farmhouses which were being used by the Germans as strong machine-gun posts. The tanks were ordered to go in first and we were to follow on behind, on foot and under heavy fire from mortars, machine guns and 88-millimetre shells, but due to an anti-tank obstruction our tanks had great difficulty in covering the ground. This, however, didn't stop them from engaging the enemies' heavy tanks. But with our tank support unable to advance we had to push forward on foot in the face of heavy German fire, which had already knocked out several of our tanks.

My company was one of the leading companies and, after a bit of a do, we took our objective, silencing the machine guns and taking many prisoners. After making certain that no Germans were left, we started to dig in. But before we'd finished this, the Germans launched a counter-attack with tanks and infantry to try and recapture the position.

The two farmhouses were about a hundred yards apart and as the German tanks came in from two directions they gave us everything they had. We had one platoon in each house and the other platoon was soon in a bad way, they had been shot up very badly and were falling back, so then our position drew all the enemy fire. We took what cover we could and, by the time the leading tank was about fifty yards away, I thought it was about time that something was done about it. And as I had the only PIAT in the platoon it was up to me to do it.

So, getting to my feet, I went forward with my PIAT and when the tank was about twenty yards away I fired one shot, which hit it just below the turret. The recoil of the PIAT knocked me flat on my back but when I got up again I saw the tank was done for. It was burning fiercely and I could hear the crackling of bullets exploding inside.

I went back to my No. 2 and reloaded my PIAT and then I saw the remaining German tanks turn tail and retire, after seeing their leader in flames. Soon after this, our tanks succeeded in over-coming obstacles and we reformed and continued our push forward.[1]

Many years later Corporal James Watts of the same 2nd Battalion, Lancashire Fusiliers, also left an account of a meeting that day with Lance-Corporal Jefferson:

I had to go to the command post where the colonel was and, whilst I was making my way back, there was a fusilier sitting down on a bit of a hill and there was a German tank that had been knocked out. I said, 'What's happened here then?' And one of the lads says, 'He's just knocked that tank out.' And I said, 'Oh, well done,' and just pushed on to deliver me message and I stayed in the command post for about half an hour. Whilst there, I heard the colonel and my company commander, Major Delaney, and they were discussing something. I was trying not to be nosy, shut me ears but I couldn't help it, and years later it dawned on me what they were talking about. They were compiling the citation for the man who'd knocked the tank out, and got the VC: Fusilier Jefferson.[2]

Biographical Detail: Born in Ulverston, Cumbria on 18 August 1921, Francis Arthur Jefferson was always known as 'Frank'.

He was a regular soldier in the British Army in 1942–6 and then secondly in 1950–1. Shortly after leaving the Army Frank went to live in the USA. He returned to Britain in the 1970s.

Francis Jefferson's Victoria Cross was stolen in January 1982 during a burglary at his mother's home at Luton Street, Bolton, Lancashire. The VC was never recovered, and its loss had a profound effect on Frank's mental health and he committed suicide while in a fit of deep depression soon after. He was cremated at Overdale Crematorium, Bolton.

LEEFE-ROBINSON, William
Rank/Service: Lieutenant, No. 39 (Home Defence) Squadron
VC Location:
Date of Gazette: 5 September 1916
Place/Date of Birth: Coorg, India, 14 July 1895
Place/Date of Death: Stanmore, London, 31 December 1918
Grave: All Saints, Harrow Weald, Middlesex
Town/County Connections: Cumbria

Account of Deed: On the night of 2/3 September 1916 over Cuffley, Hertfordshire, Lieut. Robinson, flying a converted B.E.2c night fighter, sighted a German airship – one of 16 which had left bases in Germany for a mass raid over England. The airship was the wooden-framed Schütte-Lanz SL 11, although at the time and for many years after, it was misidentified as Zeppelin L 21. Robinson made an attack at an altitude of 11,500ft (3,500m) approaching from below and closing to within 500ft (150m) raking the airship with machine-gun fire. As he was preparing for another attack, the airship burst into flames and crashed in a field behind the Plough Inn at Cuffley, killing Capt. Wilhelm Schramm and his fifteen-man crew.

Biographical Detail: William Robinson was born in Coorg, India, on 14 July 1895, the youngest son of Horace Robinson and Elizabeth Leefe. Raised on his parents' coffee estate, Kaima Betta Estate, at Pollibetta, in Coorg, he attended Bishop Cotton Boys' School, Bangalore, and the Dragon School, Oxford, before following his elder brother Harold to St Bees School, Cumbria, in September 1909. While there he succeeded his brother as head of Eaglesfield House in 1913, played in the Rugby 1st XV and became a sergeant in the school Officer Training Corps.

In August 1914 he entered the Royal Military College, Sandhurst and was gazetted into the Worcestershire Regiment in December. In March 1915 he went to France as an observer with the Royal Flying Corps, to which he had transferred. After having been wounded over Lille he underwent pilot training in Britain, before being attached to No. 39 (Home

Defence) Squadron, a night-flying squadron at Sutton's Farm Airfield near Hornchurch in Essex.

William's action in shooting down the zeppelin was witnessed by thousands of Londoners who, as they saw the airship descend in flames, cheered and sang the national anthem, one even played the bagpipes. The excitement was to last for days: long before dawn hundreds of sightseers set out for Cuffley to view the wreckage. The propaganda value of this success was enormous to the British Government, as it indicated that the German airship threat could be countered.

The authorities were not prepared for the reaction of the public. The 'prize money' which began to pour in, along with the thousands of letters and telegrams, made Robinson suddenly wealthy, and the amounts involved soon began to embarrass the War Office. Orders were passed forbidding pilots from accepting such prize money in future.

After the investiture came the other rewards. Colonel Joseph Cowen proprietor of the *Newcastle Daily Chronicle* presented Robinson with £2,000. Lord Michelham of the Bankers Herbert Stern contributed another £1,000. £500 came from William Bow, a Paisley shipbuilder, another £500 from L. A. Oldfield Esq. Robinson was presented with a silver cup by the residents of Hornchurch for which close on 300 subscriptions had been raised, and with a gold watch by the members of the Overseas Club. Messrs G Wigley and J Ball donated £100, and many smaller gifts were received. Shortly afterwards Robinson treated himself to a new Vauxhall car with some of his prize money.

It was at this time that Robinson announced his engagement to Mrs Joan Whipple, widow of Captain Herbert Connell Whipple of the Devonshire Regiment. Joan was working in a Surrey post office, but visited Sutton's Farm frequently with some friends from her days at Bentley Priory in Stanmore. Considering Robinson had so many admirers, there must have been something very special about Mrs Whipple. None of Robinson's letters to her from Germany survive, but he refers to her as 'the best girl on God's earth' in a letter to his parents.

The investiture at Windsor Castle on Friday 9 September 1916 was an occasion for more crowds. The *Daily Mail* of 10 September 1916 carried the following report:

THE KING AND VC AIRMAN

The King decorated Lieutenant William Leefe Robinson, of the Royal Flying Corps, with the Victoria Cross yesterday at Windsor Castle. The motor-car of the Zeppelin-slaying hero broke down at Runnymede and he arrived late for the investiture. The royal carriage that had awaited him in the yard of Windsor Station had gone away. 'In a fearful fright,' as he remarked to a friend, he motored into the palace yard. After affixing the Victoria Cross and very warmly congratulating Lieutenant Robinson on his gallant feat, the King, interposing constant questions which displayed his keen technical interest in aviation, extracted from him a long and detailed account of how he brought down the Zeppelin. His Majesty produced a fine collection of photographs, taken from aeroplanes in France, which have been sent to him by the Prince of Wales. After talking long and warmly of France and the French air service, the King expressed the opinion that the British and French airmen are infinitely superior to those of the enemy. The King asked Lieutenant Robinson questions about his father and grandfather, and recalled that his grandfather Mr. William Braham Robinson was once chief constructor at Portsmouth Dockyard.

Although he arrived late, Robinson found hundreds of people waiting to catch a glimpse of him entering and leaving the castle. He would have to face many such crowds in the months ahead, and donning civilian clothes was no protection. His face was everywhere. In some households there was a picture of him in every room!

In April 1917, Robinson was posted to France as a Flight Commander with No. 48 Squadron, flying the then new Bristol F.2 Fighter. On the first patrol over the lines, Robinson's formation of six aircraft encountered the Albatross D.III fighters of Jasta 11, led by Manfred von Richthofen (the 'Red Baron'), and four were shot down. Robinson, shot down by *Vizefeldwebel* Sebastian Festner, was wounded and captured. He was imprisoned at Zorndorfand Holzminden. As a highly decorated prisoner of war he was not well treated by the Germans. He made several attempts to escape but all failed, and was kept in solitary confinement at the latter camp for his escape attempts; his health was badly affected during his time as a POW.

Robinson survived the war, but by the time the Armistice was declared (November 1918) Karl Niemeyer, the Commandant at Holzminden POW camp, had very nearly succeeded in breaking his spirit.

William Robinson was shipped back to Scotland as soon as he was fit enough to travel and landed in Leith on 14 December 1918. From a camp in Yorkshire he was granted leave until February 1919. On 23 December 1918, Captain William Leefe-Robinson VC returned to Harrow Weald to spend Christmas with his friends the Cliftons, though he still needed to use a walking stick to aid his sickly body.

That winter saw the country in the clutches of one of the world's worst influenza epidemics – the Spanish Flu. Worldwide 27,000,000 died. In England alone some 150,000 were struck down.

In his less than healthy state, Robinson succumbed to the infection and his sister Kitty, by then Baroness Heyking, and his fiancée Joan, nursed him as best they could but he no longer had the strength to fight his illness. On Tuesday, 31 December 1918, William's condition quickly deteriorated.

During the delirium which preceded his last moments, Captain Robinson was haunted by the vision of the arch-brute. He imagined that Niemeyer and sentries with fixed bayonets were standing by his deathbed. Several times he called out to be protected from the fiend.

He died later that night (31 December 1918) from cardiac failure at the Stanmore home of his sister. He was only 23 years old. He was the first person to be awarded the VC for action in the UK.

He was buried at All Saints' churchyard extension in Harrow Weald. A memorial to him was later erected near the spot where the airship crashed. This was renovated in 1986 and again in 2009, the latter occasion being to correct movement of the obelisk and surrounding footpath caused by subsidence.

An additional monument was erected in East Ridgeway, unveiled on 9 June 1921, and by a road named after him (Robinson Close) in Hornchurch, Essex, on the site of the former Sutton's Farm airfield. A short segment of a wartime newsreel survives although the location and date of the recorded event were unknown.

He was also commemorated by the name of the local Miller & Carter steakhouse just south of the cemetery, the Leefe-Robinson VC, on the Uxbridge Road, Harrow Weald.

In April 2010, to celebrate the 100th anniversary of the Great Northern Route extension that connects Grange Park to Cuffley, the First Capital Connect rail company named a Class 313 train *Captain William Leefe-Robinson VC*.

Captain William Leefe-Robinson's Victoria Cross medal was passed on to his sister Katherine Baroness Heyking and after her death was passed on to her daughter Regina (Mrs Regina G Libin). Strangely, his other Great War medals were in the hands of another private individual (Roy Bartlett). On 22 November 1988 all the medals and other memorabilia were brought together at Christie's in London. Mrs Regina G Libin auctioned all the medals and memorabilia and raised £99,000 on behalf of 'A Medal for Life', a charitable trust to benefit children suffering from leukaemia.

Finally, the propeller from the plane Leefe-Robinson was flying when he shot down the airship is on public display in the Armoury of Culzean Castle in Ayrshire. It was given to the Marquess of Ailsa in thanks for letting his land at Turnberry be used for an RFC flying school.

MAYSON, Tom Fletcher
Rank/Service: Lance-Sergeant, 4th Bn King's Own (Royal) Lancaster
   Regiment
VC Location: King's Own Royal Regiment Museum, Lancaster
Date of Gazette: 14 September 1917
Place/Date of Birth: Silecroft, 3 November 1893
Place/Date of Death: Barrow-in-Furness, Cumbria, 21 February 1958
Grave: St Mary's churchyard, Wicham
Town/County Connections: Coniston; Ulverston, Cumbria

Account of Deed: On 31 July 1917 at Wieltje, Belgium, when his platoon was
held up by machine-gun fire, Lance-Sergeant Mayson, without waiting for
orders, at once made for the gun which he put out of action with bombs,
wounding four of the team; the remaining three of the team fled, pursued
by Lance-Sergeant Mayson to a dug-out where he killed them. Later, when
clearing up a strongpoint, this NCO again tackled a machine-gun single-
handed, killing six of the team. Finally during an enemy counter-attack
he took charge of an isolated post and successfully held it until ordered to
withdraw when his ammunition was exhausted.

Biographical Detail: Tom Fletcher Mayson was born on 3 November
1893 in the John Bull Inn at Silecroft in Cumberland. He enlisted on 16
November 1914, served throughout the war with 1/4th King's Own and
was wounded twice.

   On Saturday 1 December 1917 Tom Mayson returned to Millom and
Silecroft after receiving his Victoria Cross from HM the King at Buckingham
Palace three days earlier. At a special ceremony in Silecroft Tom Mayson was
presented with a gold watch, chain and medal and an illuminated address.
The watch, a handsome demi-hunter, bore a monogram on the outer case,
while inside was the inscription, 'Presented to Lance Sergeant Tom F
Mayson, KORL Regt., with hearty congratulations and best wishes from the
parishioners of Whicham and Furness on receiving the VC, September 19th,
1917'. The chain, a massive gold cable, was adorned with a choice medallion in
gold and enamel of the badge of the King's Own Royal Lancaster Regiment.

Tom Mayson died on 21 February 1958 and is buried in Whicham churchyard, Silecroft. His Victoria Cross was left to Whicham church from where it is on loan to the regimental museum to be displayed alongside his other medals. The 'Silecroft' gold chain and medal were acquired by the museum in October 2010.

SMITH, Edward 'Ned' Benn

Rank/Service: Sergeant (later Lieutenant), Lancashire Fusiliers

Other Decorations: DCM

VC Location:

Date of Gazette: 22 October 1918

Place/Date of Birth: 1 North Quay, Maryport, Cumbria, 10 November 1899

Place/Date of Death: France, 12 January 1940

Grave: Beuvry Communal Cemetery, France

Town/County Connections: Maryport, Cumbria

Significant Remarks: Edward Smith, at 19, was the youngest soldier of the First World War to be awarded the Victoria Cross. He is also unusual in having gained both the DCM and VC, and in quick succession, during the Hundred Days Offensive.

Account of Deed: On 21–3 August 1918, as a sergeant in the Lancashire Fusiliers while in command of a platoon, he took a machine-gun post with a rifle and bayonet and killed six enemy soldiers. Later he led his men to help another platoon in trouble, took command and captured the objective. During a counter-attack the next day he helped to restore a portion of the line.

Biographical Details: Born Edward Benn Smith in November 1899 at the home of his parents, 1 North Quay located beside Maryport harbour, Edward was known familiarly as 'Ned' throughout his life. In 1917 he left his job as a coal miner at the Oughterside Colliery and joined the Lancashire Fusiliers at the age of 18. In little more than year, Ned Smith had been promoted to the rank of sergeant and been awarded both the Distinguished Conduct Medal (DCM) for separate actions of bravery[3] over a period of a few days in August 1918 and the Victoria Cross. The action for which he won his VC took place on his nineteenth birthday which made him the youngest soldier of the First World War to be awarded the Victoria Cross. His VC action took place a mere eleven days after the DCM events.

According to the *Whitehaven News,* a local West Cumbrian newspaper, when Smith returned home after the Great War in 1919, he was greeted by a jubilant and cheering crowd of 6,000 people: at the time this was equal to the total population of Maryport.

Ned remained in the Army and served for a further twenty-one years in China, Malaya and Ireland before retiring with an army pension in 1938 having attained the rank of Regimental Sergeant-Major. He then joined the Corps of Commissionaires in London for about a year. However, with war becoming increasingly likely by the summer of 1939, Ned Smith re-enlisted with his former regiment.

In the Second World War with the rank of Lieutenant (Quartermaster) Edward Benn Smith, VC, DCM (service No. 107894) served with the 2nd Battalion, Lancashire Fusiliers, which was among the first of the British Expeditionary Force (BEF) to be sent to France. Unfortunately, members of the Lancashire Fusiliers were some of the earliest casualties of the war and these included Ned, who died on 12 January 1940 at the age of 41 (possibly due to friendly fire, five months before the start of the Battle of France in May).

On Saturday 13 January, Ned's parents Mr and Mrs C. Smith received the dreaded official telegram informing them their only son had been 'killed in Action'. He had died from injuries caused by a head wound the previous day.

In addition to the official telegram, his mother and father received the following communication from their son's Colonel in France.

13 January 1940
Dear Mr and Mrs Smith,
   I have the dreadful task of informing you that your son Edward, passed away as a result of a bullet wound in the head and was buried with full military honours this afternoon. His death has stunned us all and we deeply feel the loss of a gallant officer. He was a tower of strength to the battalion and a friend of every officer and man. I can hardly express to you our profound grief and heartfelt sympathy. The

sole comfort is that he died very soon after he received the fatal wound and suffered hardly any pain. God rest his soul and comfort you both.

He was buried at the Beuvry Communal Cemetery Extension (Plot 1, Row B). Ned Smith never married.

A memorial plaque was placed outside his parents' home at North Quay, Maryport, but was moved to the town's Christ Church at the request of his parents who said it was being vandalised. After the closure of Christ Church it was moved to St Mary's church.

SMITH, James Alexander
Rank/Service: Private, King's Own (Royal) Border Regiment
VC Location: Border Regiment Museum, Carlisle Castle
Date of Gazette: 18 February 1915
Place/Date of Birth: Workington, Cumbria, 5 January 1881
Place/Date of Death: 73 Thorntree Avenue, Brambles Farm, Middlesbrough,
   May 1968
Grave: Acklam Cemetery, Middlesbrough
Town/County Connections: Middlesbrough; Workington Cumbria

Account of Deed: On 21 December 1914 at Rouges Bancs, France, Smith
and Abraham Acton VC voluntarily went out from their trench and rescued
a wounded man who had been lying exposed against the enemy's trenches
for fifteen hours. On the same day they again left their trench under heavy
fire to bring in another wounded man. They were under fire for sixty
minutes whilst conveying the wounded men to safety.

Biographical Detail: Born James Alexander Glenn on 5 January 1881 in the
parish of St Michael's, Workington, Cumbria: he is thought to have taken
his mother's maiden name so he could enlist at the age of 13 into the 3rd
Militia Battalion at Carlisle.

He was discharged on 3 January 1900 having completed his term of
service and then re-enlisted on 12 March 1906, being discharged on 11
March 1910. He re-enlisted at the outbreak of the war and rejoined 3rd
(Special Reserve) Battalion in August 1914 having been called up from
Middlesbrough.

Posted overseas with a draft of reinforcements to the 2nd Battalion on 25
November 1914, he joined the Battalion on the front line on 2 December
1914.

In March 1915, three months after his courageous acts, he was wounded
and returned to Workington. The *West Cumberland Times* recorded how Pte
Smith arrived home by the last train from Carlisle, trying to avoid a fuss.

That he did not manage entirely to avoid the welcome waiting for him was due to his being 'spotted' on the train at Wigton. The news was wired on to Maryport and from Maryport to Workington and when he appeared his modesty was shocked by the reception.

He found himself taken prisoner and hoisted shoulder high before he left the booking hall and he narrowly escaped being carried in triumph through the streets. The artillerymen and band had not heard of his 'second coming' in time and the borough fathers had definitely abandoned hope of surprising him so these were not there. But the others were numerous and amid congratulatory greetings of all sorts he was carried like the hero that he has proved himself, to his father's house in Southey Street.

The newspaper reported that 'an attempt to get him to say a few words at one of the halls as a stimulus to recruiting was fruitless. He could a tale unfold, but he doesn't because he isn't built that way. He has apparently recovered from the wound he received at Chapelle, and he looks fit and capable.'

The Duke Street Mission Hall and the surrounding streets were crowded when Workington's mayor, Alderman P Walls made a presentation to the hero. The paper records that 'on the platform beside him were Pte Smith and his aged father, and supporting them Lt Col Nash, the officer commanding the Border Depot, Colonel Sparrow, aldermen and members of the Corporation, and the Town Clerk'.

The proceedings opened with the national anthem and the mayor told the audience: 'I knew James Smith (Jimmy) when only a youth, a modest, lively, fine fellow. He was born on the Marsh, one of our workers, and I think everybody in Workington feels honoured by Pte James Smith's honour on the battlefield.'

To loud and prolonged applause, the mayor presented Pte Smith with a medal and a purse containing 25 sovereigns and the audience sang 'For He's a Jolly Good Fellow'.

The newspaper states:

Pte Smith, modest and hesitant replied: 'Well ladies and gentlemen, I am very pleased that Workington has seen fit to honour me. I thank them all – the council and the people of Workington who have thought so much of me. To one and all I am "yours truly" a chip off the old block (loud applause).'

Lieutenant Colonel Nash said he hoped that Pte Smith's example would be an inducement to many more to come forward and enlist; but Col Sparrow said he was sorry to see that young men were not responding as they might do. They were going about with little bunches of red, white and blue ribbons in their buttonholes; which, he said, was very pretty but it was not what they wanted.

The newspaper described the scene as the ceremony ended:

Outside a dense crowd waited until Pte Smith appeared. He was instantly surrounded and amid the hat waving and cheering he had to shake innumerable hands and only with difficulty could the police make a way for him out of the street and towards his home.

The following day, Pte Smith left Workington for London to receive his medal from King George V.

The *West Cumberland Times* reported that: 'His Majesty shook hands with him and spoke a few words of cordial congratulations.'

While on leave in 1915 Private James Smith (or Glenn) VC married early in May at North Ormesby parish church near Middlesbrough Miss Eliza Reynolds of Stovin Street, Middlesbrough, where the bridegroom resided before the war.

Later, at a recruiting rally, Pte Smith was presented with 'purses of gold' on behalf of the Ironmasters' Association, the blast-furnace men (he had worked in the trade before the war) and members of the corporation.

He served overseas until January 1917, returned to England and was finally discharged on 8 January 1919. After the war, he went back to Middlesbrough where he served with the Home Guard during the Second World War and died in May 1968 at the age of 88. His medals were bequeathed to the Border Regiment and are on display in the regimental museum at Carlisle Castle. He is named on the VC Memorial, Town Hall, Middlesbrough, and on the VC Memorial Carlisle Cathedral.

WASSALL, Samuel
Rank/Service: Private, 80th Regiment (South Staffordshire)
VC Location: Staffordshire Regiment Museum, Lichfield
Date of Gazette: 17 June 1879
Place/Date of Birth: Birmingham, 28 July 1856
Place/Date of Death: Barrow-in-Furness, Cumbria, 4 February 1927
Grave: Barrow-in-Furness Cemetery, section 3B, Plot 1952 (headstone erected 1985)
Town/County Connections: Birmingham; Barrow-in-Furness, Cumbria

Account of Deed: At the Battle of Isandhlwana, Zululand, South Africa, on 22 January 1879, at the imminent risk of his own life, Private Wassall saved that of Private Westwood, of the same regiment when the camp at Isandhlwana on the Tufela River, about 10 miles from Rorke's Drift, was attacked and taken by the enemy. Private Wassall retreated towards the Tufela River, in which he saw a comrade struggling, and apparently drowning. He rode to the bank, dismounted, leaving his horse on the Zulu side, rescued the man from the stream, and again mounted his horse, dragging Private Westwood across the river under a heavy shower of bullets.

Biographical Detail: Wassall is believed to have been born at 11 The Court, Alcester Street, Aston, on 28 July 1856, the son of Thomas a wire-maker and Elizabeth (née Silk). He worked as an apprentice dyer before joining the 80th Regiment (Staffordshire Volunteers), later the South Staffs Regiment, at Dudley on 26 November 1874.

He was only 22 when the camp at Isandhlwana was overrun by Zulus. It was one of the blackest days in army history, with 1,300 troops slaughtered by Zulus and the bravery of the survivors was highlighted in film *Zulu Dawn*: he was the youngest man in the British Army at that time to win the VC.

Private Wassall was always proud to take his place with ex-servicemen on ceremonial occasions at which the military were present. He attended the unveiling of the cenotaph in Barrow Public Park by General Sir William Robertson, who shook hands with Private Wassall and congratulated him.

On this and subsequent Armistice Days Private Wassall was invariably asked to place the ex-servicemen's laurel wreath on the memorial. He was one of several other Barrow members who were introduced to the King at Furness Abbey station when His Majesty, with the Queen, visited Barrow on 17 May 1917.

In July 1920, he was present at a reception by the King and Queen at Buckingham Palace, which, he afterwards declared, was one of the greatest experiences of his life. It was his first visit to London, but the third time on which he had shaken hands with the King.

After leaving the Army, Wassall settled in Barrow-in-Furness where he worked as a dockyard electrician.

Covered with the flag he loved so well, and fought so bravely for, the mortal remains of Mr. Samuel Wassall, Barrow's VC, who died in the North Lonsdale Hospital in his 70th year, were laid to rest in Barrow Cemetery on Thursday afternoon. Leaving from his home at 34, Lyon Street, Barrow where he had resided for 46 years, the people of Barrow, quietly and reverently paid their last tribute to the gallant old gentleman, and even his comrades at Lichfield, the headquarters of his old regiment, were represented by Sergeant F. Smith, 2nd Bn South Stafford's Regiment.

The chief mourners were his widow, four sons and three daughters; Mr. and Mrs. Samuel Wassall, Mr. and Mrs. Albery Wassall, Mr. and Mrs. Ernest Wassall and Mr. Henry Wassall, sons and daughters-in-law; Mr. and Mrs. Sutton, Mr. and Mrs. Leonard, Mr. and Mrs. E. Huddard, daughters and sons-in-law; Mr. Albert and Mr. George Wassall; nephews; Mr. George and Mr. Herbert Sutton; grandchildren.[4]

WESTON, William Basil
Rank/Service: Lieutenant, 1st Bn West Yorkshire (Prince of Wales Own) Regiment
VC Location:
Date of Gazette: 15 May 1945
Place/Date of Birth: Ulverston, Cumbria, 3 January 1924
Place/Date of Death: Meiktila, Burma, 3 March 1945
Grave: Tauukkyan War Cemetery, Burma
Town/County Connections: Ulverston, Cumbria

Account of Deed: On 3 March 1945 during an attack on Meiktila, Burma, Lieutenant Weston was commanding a platoon which, together with the rest of the company, had to clear an area of the town of the enemy. In the face of fanatical opposition he led his men superbly, encouraging them from one bunker position to the next. When he came to the last, particularly well-defended bunker, he led a party with bayonets and grenades to eliminate the enemy within the bunker. At the entrance, he fell forward wounded. As he lay injured, he pulled the pin from a grenade and by so doing killed himself and most of the enemy in the bunker. Throughout the final three and a half hours of the battle, he set an example which can seldom have been equalled.

Biographical Detail: Born in Cumbrian town of Ulverston, at the age of 21 Lieutenant Weston joined the Green Howards in 1943, was commissioned the following year and having completed his jungle training was posted to the West Yorkshire's in December 1944; within three months he was killed in action.

WYATT, George Harry
Rank/Service: Lance-Corporal (later L-Sgt), 3rd Bn, Coldstream Guards
Other Decorations:
VC Location: Private (not on public display)
Date of Gazette: 18 November 1915
Place/Date of Birth: Worcester, 5 September 1886
Place/Date of Death: Doncaster, Yorkshire, 22 January 1964
Grave: Cadeby Churchyard, near Doncaster, South Yorkshire
Memorials:
Town/County Connections: Worcester; Doncaster, Yorks; Whitehaven,
  Cumbria

Account of Deed: On 25/26 August 1914 at Landrecies, France, part of
Lance-Corporal Wyatt's battalion was hotly engaged close to some farm
buildings, when the enemy set alight some straw sacks in the farmyard. The
Lance-Corporal twice dashed out under very heavy fire from the enemy,
only 25 yards away, and extinguished the burning straw, making it possible
to hold the position. Later, although wounded in the head, he continued
firing until he could no longer see owing to the blood pouring down his
face. The medical officer bound up his wound and ordered him to the rear,
but he returned to the firing line and continued fighting.

Biographical Detail: George Henry Wyatt, the son of a groom, was born
in Worcester on 5 September 1886. After attending Holloway School at
Droitwich, Wyatt enlisted in the Coldstream Guards at Birmingham on 23
November 1904. He served with the 2nd Battalion at home, and with the
3rd Battalion in Egypt. After serving in Egypt for two and a half years, he
left the British Army in November 1904.

Wyatt joined the Barnsley Police Force and later transferred to the
Doncaster Borough Police. He married Ellen Wyatt (née Graham) of Kells,
a coal miner's daughter, at Christ Church, Whitehaven, in 1912 and the
couple had two children. Mrs Wyatt came back to Whitehaven to live with
her parents at Kells while her husband was serving abroad.

Wyatt was recalled to the colours on the outbreak of the First World War as a reservist. He rejoined the 3rd Battalion Coldstream Guards and as a member of the British Expeditionary Force left for France on 14 August 1914.

Soon after arriving on the Western Front Wyatt took part in the Battle of Mons. On two occasions he displayed outstanding bravery and was awarded the Victoria Cross. It was presented to him at Buckingham Palace on 4 March 1916. Wyatt returned to France and on 28 February was promoted to Lance-Sergeant. He was wounded on two occasions.

Wyatt returned to the Doncaster constabulary in 1919 and in June 1924 bravely stopped a runaway horse. He retired from the police in February 1934 and took up farming. George Wyatt died on 22 January 1964 and is buried at Cadeby Cemetery near Doncaster.

After the war George Wyatt, was interviewed about winning the Victoria Cross:

> Well, there's not much for me to say about it. I just did as I was told. During the retirement from Mons the 3rd Coldstream Guards reached Landrecis. It was dark at the time, and there we were attacked by a large number of Germans who must have been rushed up in motor Lorries. We lost our machine-gun, and had to rely solely upon rifle and bayonet. Suddenly something flared up between us and the enemy, and Major Matheson shouted, 'Put out that light'. So I did it. I never thought it would bring me the Victoria Cross. How did I put the fire out? Oh, I jumped on it and dragged some equipment over it. After a while it burst out again, and I ran back and extinguished it. Yes, there was heavy fire from the Germans when I first obeyed the order. At that affair at Villers Cotterets. I got hit on the head and went on firing. That's all.

As well as the Victoria Cross, he was also awarded the 1914 Star and Bar, British War Medal, Victory Medal, 1937 Coronation Medal, 1953 Coronation, Russian Order of St George (3rd Class). He was also mentioned in despatches.

Cumbria Notes

1. Adapted from Roderick Bailey (in association with the Imperial War Museum), *Forgotten Voices: Victoria Cross* (Ebury Press, 2011).
2. Ibid.
3. On 10 August 1918, then a Corporal with the 1/5th Battalion, Lancashire Fusiliers, Ned Smith was leading a daylight patrol near Hebuteme in the Somme Area of France to examine points in the German lines where information was required. As the patrol was about to retire, he saw a party of about forty Germans about to take up outpost duty. Despite being heavily outnumbered by the German soldiers, Corporal Smith led his small party of men and engaged the enemy, breaking up the German party and causing severe casualties. As well as receiving the DCM for this action, Ned Smith was promoted to the rank of Lance Sergeant.
4. *Daily Mail*, 5 Feb. 1927.

Durham Victoria Cross Holders

ANDERSON, Charles

Rank / Service: Private (later Cpl), 2nd Dragoon Guards (Queen's Bays)
VC Location: 1st Queen's Dragoon Guards Museum, Cardiff
Date of Gazette: 11 November 1862
Place / Date of Birth: Liverpool, 1826
Place / Date of Death: Seaham Harbour, Sunderland, 19 April 1899
Grave: Princess Road Cemetery, Seaham, Section A, Grave 1271 (erected 1989)
Town / County Connections: Liverpool; Sunderland

Account of Deed: For saving the life of Lieutenant-Colonel Seymour CB, commanding the regiment, in an attack made on him on 8 October 1858, by mutinous sepoys, in a dense jungle of sugar canes, from which an attempt was made to dislodge them. The mutineers numbered between thirty and forty. They suddenly opened fire on Lieutenant-Colonel Seymour and his party at a few yards distance, and immediately afterwards rushed in upon them with drawn (native) swords. Pistolling a man, cutting at him and emptying with deadly effect at arm's length every barrel of his revolver, Lieutenant-Colonel Seymour was cut down by two sword cuts, when Private Charles Anderson and Trumpeter Thomas J Monaghan rushed to his rescue, and the Trumpeter shooting a man with his pistol in the act of cutting at him, and both Trumpeter and Dragoon driving at the enemy with their swords, enabled him to arise, and assist in defending himself again, when the whole of the enemy were despatched. The occurrence took place soon after the action fought near Sundeela, Oudh.

Biographical Detail: Following his discharge from the Army, by which time he had achieved the rank of corporal, Charles Anderson settled at Seaham, where sadly he died of a fractured skull following a fall from cliffs near his home, Swinbank Cottage, Seaham Harbour.

ANNAND, Richard Wallace
Rank/Service: 2nd Lieutenant (later Capt.), 2nd Bn, Durham Light Infantry
VC Location: Durham Light Infantry Museum, Durham
Date of Gazette: 23 August 1940
Place/Date of Birth: South Shields, Co. Durham, 5 November 1914
Place/Date of Death: University Hospital, Durham, 24 December 2004
Grave: Durham City Crematorium
Memorials: Statue Vestibule, South Shields Town Hall[1]
Town/County Connections: South Shields, Co. Durham

Significant Remarks: The first Army VC of the Second World War.[2]

Account of Deed: For most conspicuous gallantry on 15/16 May 1940 when the platoon under his command was on the south side of the River Dyle, astride a blown bridge. During the night, a strong attack was beaten off, but about 11.00am, the enemy again launched a violent attack and pushed forward a bridging party into the sunken bottom of the river. 2nd Lieutenant Annand attacked this party, but when ammunition ran out, he went forward himself over open ground, with total disregard for enemy mortar and machine-gun fire. Reaching the top of the bridge, he drove out the party below, inflicting over twenty casualties with hand grenades. Having been wounded he rejoined his platoon, had his wound dressed, and then carried on in command. During the evening, another attack was launched and again 2nd Lieutenant Annand went forward with hand grenades and inflicted heavy casualties on the enemy. When the order to withdraw was received, he withdrew his platoon, but learning on the way back that his batman was wounded and had been left behind, he returned at once to the former position and brought him back in a wheelbarrow, before losing consciousness as the result of wounds.

Biographical Detail: Richard Wallace Annand was born in South Shields, Co. Durham, on 5 November 1914.[3] His parents were Wallace Moir Annand and Dora Elizabeth Chapman. He was only seven months old when his father was killed in action. Lieutenant-Commander Annand died while serving with the Collingwood Battalion of the Royal Naval Division at Gallipoli in June 1915.

The young Richard, known as 'Dick' or 'Dickie', was educated at Pocklington School in East Yorkshire, where he was a boarder. After leaving in 1933, he joined the National Provincial Bank and worked in branches in South Shields, Rugby and London.

Dickie Annand had wanted to follow his father into the Royal Navy and, as a first step, in October 1933 became a midshipman in the Tyne Division of the Royal Naval Volunteer Reserve. He was promoted to the rank of Sub-lieutenant in 1936. The following year the bank transferred him to a branch in London so that he could continue his RNVR service on HMS *President* on the Thames. He attended a navigation course at Portsmouth and a gunnery course at Whale Island, as well as taking part in exercises at sea. Annand applied for a regular commission in the Royal Navy but was told that he was too old – this was a heavy blow, as all his life he had wanted to be a naval officer. He was offered an administrative position but turned this down and decided to try the Army instead.

He was accepted for a regular commission in the Army and left his bank job. In January 1938, he was gazetted as a 2nd Lieutenant with the Supplementary Reserve of the Durham Light Infantry (DLI). After a period of training, Annand was attached to the 2nd Battalion DLI.

Annand received his VC from King George VI in the Grand Hall of Buckingham Palace on 3 September 1940. The investiture was held inside the Palace instead of the Quadrangle, as there was an air-raid alert at the time. Despite the threatened air raid, huge crowds gathered outside the Palace to see the heroes leave after receiving their decorations.

On the day he received his VC Richard Annand became engaged to Miss Shirley Osborne, and they were married at St George's, Hanover Square, London, in November that year; it was a happy marriage that lasted sixty-four years and they celebrated their diamond wedding anniversary on 9 November 2000.

2nd Lieutenant Annand was awarded the freedom of the borough at South Shields at a ceremony in November 1940. The Harton Colliery band played 'See the Conquering Hero Comes' as 2,000 onlookers cheered. In his speech of thanks, Annand said:

> I have been lucky, extremely lucky. I thank God for that luck, but I would like you to know there were others who ought to have the award as well as me. Countless deeds have been done that have gone unrewarded. Every one of the men with me there deserves a medal. When I received this award my feelings were of a communal satisfaction and not an individual one.

After being invalided back to England, Annand rejoined the reformed 2nd Battalion at Bridlington, East Yorkshire, but was never again fit enough for active service. In June 1941, as a result of rifle practice on the ranges, he lost what remained of his hearing and was discharged from the battalion. He learned to lip-read and fought to stay in the Army.

In September, he was appointed instructor at the Commando Training Centre in Inverness. He was promoted to Temporary Captain in October 1941, and in January 1942 was posted to the DLI Training Battalion in Co. Durham. The following month he took up a new post in Elgin training the local Home Guard. He was then seconded to Gordonstoun School to instruct cadets in pre-service training, followed by an appointment as instructor at the Highland Fieldcraft Centre in the Cairngorms. His last posting of the war was to the War Office in London. After being offered a commission in the Pay Corps, which he declined, he was invalided out of the Army, due to severe deafness, in December 1948. He retained his rank of Captain.

Because of his loss of hearing, he had a natural affinity with disabled people, particularly the deaf, and in 1949 Annand found his vocation. He was appointed Personnel Officer at Finchale Abbey Training Centre for the handicapped in Co. Durham. Many of the thousands who passed through the centre ended up in regular employment thanks to his dedication and hard work. Captain Annand remained there until his retirement in 1980 at the age of 65. He was a founder member of the British Association for the Hard of Hearing – now Hearing Concern.

In 1956, he was appointed a Deputy Lieutenant for Co. Durham and he was President of the Durham Branch of the Light Infantry Club until 1998.

In addition to the VC, Annand received the 1939–45 Star, Defence Medal, War Medal 1939–45, Coronation Medal 1953, Silver Jubilee Medal 1977, Golden Jubilee Medal 2002 and the Army Emergency Reserve Decoration & Bar. The VC group is now on display at the DLI Museum, Durham City.

He proved his courage again in 1979 when he saved his wife from drowning. They had just attended dinner aboard HMS *Bacchante*, anchored in the River Tyne, when Mrs Annand fell from the gang plank into the river. Captain Annand immediately jumped in to support his wife until they were both lifted out of the water by the ship's crew.

He was present at the VC Centenary Review by HM the Queen in Hyde Park, London, in June 1956 and attended the first dinner of the VC and GC Association at the Café Royal, London in July 1958. He took part in many VC and George Cross reunions and was one of the eleven VC recipients at the dedication of the VC and GC Memorial in Westminster Abbey in May 2003.

Captain Annand VC died, at the age of 90, in the University Hospital of North Durham on Christmas Eve 2004. He was survived by his wife Shirley. The couple had no children. His funeral was held at St Cuthbert's church, North Road, Durham on 5 January 2005.[4] A memorial service was held at Durham Cathedral on 7 February. General Sir Peter de la Billiere, formerly of the DLI, gave a reading from *Pilgrim's Progress* and the standards of Durham Light Infantry Association branches were paraded through the Cathedral. More than 1,000 people had come to pay tribute to Richard Annand's wartime heroism and his devotion to helping the disabled.

Today, there are many personal testimonies and eyewitness accounts preserved in the archives of the Imperial War Museum that make interesting reading. In respect of Annand's deeds, here are just a few reports concerning his actions that day, beginning with his own account:

I was on the Supplementary Reserve when the war started. The function of the Supplementary Reserve was to fill the vacancies for junior officers in the regular battalion in the event of war, and so, as soon as the war began, I went straight to the Second Battalion who I'd done my training with the previous year. I was very enthusiastic. I felt that it justified all the training that one had attempted to do and it was certainly a chance to try to make some little contribution towards the task of defeating the enemy.

Having rejoined the battalion at Woking, I went out with it, on 25 September, to France. We crossed to Cherbourg from Southampton and after a week we were transported by train to the Franco–Belgian frontier, where we remained during the Phoney War for some eight or nine months. While there we were engaged practically all the time in digging what was known as the Gort Line, which was the northern continuation of the Maginot Line.

On the evening before the German attack commenced, we had been into Douai for the purposes of watching a show in a theatre. At the end of it, we returned to Nomain and during the night I was called out by the company commander to take a detachment to go and search for German parachutists who were reported to have come down in the area. I took my platoon out and we didn't actually find any parachutists. It was possibly a false alarm, I don't know, but anyway we were very soon aware of the German planes that were flying over. They had been over our position and bombing our rear areas, where our supplies were, further back behind the lines.

We then managed to get right up to take up a position on the River Dyle, in Belgium, which had been planned some time before. We were taken by transport from our positions in the Nomain area over the border, through Tournai and up near Waterloo actually: where we fought on the Dyle was within five miles of Waterloo. Anyway, we got up to our positions on the Dyle without any harassment from the enemy. We met a lot of Belgian soldiers coming back towards us down the line who had been up there before and we took over from them.

Our company was on the west bank, with the Dyle flowing northwards, with the company headquarters and the other companies distributed in the area. We were told that the Germans wouldn't be arriving for at least another week. In fact they arrived the day after we did.

Lance Corporal James Miller, 2nd Battalion, Durham Light Infantry:

It was getting dusk and the Germans were trying to get a pontoon across the bridge: they were trying to get across. We had grenades there, like, and Annand, he had a sandbag, and he said, 'Put some grenades in this,' and I put about half a dozen in and he went out and he was slinging hand grenades at the Jerries trying to get the pontoon across the bridge. He came back again and I put some more in for him, some more hand grenades. I think he went out three times. He was a brave man.

Sergeant Major Martin McLane, 2nd Battalion, Durham Light Infantry:

How that man never got hit with all the shooting going on, I don't ever know. It was a miracle, really. I say this honestly, not because I know the man now and we're great friends. He ran across this bridge with his grenades, dodging here and there, ducking and skipping down, moving around, and he got to the edge of this bridge and he just unloaded his grenades and he came back. He caused devastation in that area. I don't know who was in there but you could hear them yelling, you know. Don't think that a soldier dies peacefully, they yell when they're hit, the wounded; they scream for their mothers, a lot of them; and you could hear the screams coming from the place of men badly hit. The dead wouldn't have anything to say about it all – they were out of it. And then the Germans attacked again and they got another bridging party in and he did the same thing again with his grenades. He went over again and attacked this position and he destroyed the German post there – it was reputed after the war that he'd killed forty Germans – and the Germans stopped all work on trying to support that bridge. He got wounded on his way back.

Lance Corporal James Miller, 2nd Battalion, Durham Light Infantry:

> Then we got the order to move out. We had to get out of the position, we had to get out quick, and we went up a road and a roll call was made and Sergeant O'Neill, I think it was, said to him, 'Sir, your batman's missing. Joe Hunter, he's back there.' And Lieutenant Annand went back for him and he found a barrow in a barn, there was barn to the right of the trench we'd been in and he found a wheelbarrow in there, and he got Joe back, he wheeled him. That's why they called him 'The Wheelbarrow VC'. Joe was taken to some hospital but later on the hospital was overrun by the Germans and he was took prisoner, but his legs had gone and he died in a prisoner of war camp.

Sergeant T O'Neil wrote his account of Annand's actions in the *Journal* and *Northern Mail*, and this personal view gives a more complete picture.

> On the night of 15 May, Mr. Annand came to me at platoon headquarters and asked for a box of grenades as he could hear Jerry trying to repair the bridge. Off he went, and he sure must have given them a lovely time because it wasn't a great while before he was back for more. Just like giving an elephant strawberries.
>
> The previous night, while the heavy stuff of both sides were sending over their mutual regards, he realized that he had not received word from our right forward section which held a pillbox about 250 yards to our right front, so he went out to see how they were fixed. He had gone about two hours and we had come to the conclusion that they had got him when something which I found hard to recognize came crawling in. It was just Jake – that is the name by which we knew him. He looked as though he had been having an argument with a wild cat. His clothes were tom to shreds and he was cut and bruised all over.

How he got there and back only he knows, because he had the fire of our own troops to contend with as well as Jerry's. I don't suppose he knows the meaning of fear. He never asked a man to do anything he could do himself. He wouldn't talk much about it. He wasn't that kind. It was just another job of work for him.

Another platoon of Royal Welsh Fusiliers came to reinforce us and had been there only half an hour when one of our own mortar bombs dropped right among them. Jake came dashing up, asked me what had happened and then off he went, galloping up the hillside to stop the mortar platoon. He didn't even stop to take his steel helmet and he was under fire all the way.

Sergeant Major Martin McLane, 2nd Battalion, Durham Light Infantry:

He found his batman and he put him in a wheelbarrow and wheeled him up this rugged track, and when he caught up with the troops he collapsed with loss of blood. Well, everybody tabbed on to that and called him 'The Wheelbarrow VC' but King's Regulations state quite firmly, 'An officer who hazards his life for to save a junior rank will not be eligible for an award.' It's the wrong interpretation of him getting the VC entirely, because it was for the brave deed of bombing them Germans when they were bridging.

2nd Lieutenant Richard Annand, 2nd Battalion, Durham Light Infantry:

They saw I was wounded with blood all over and I was ordered by the adjutant into a vehicle to be taken to hospital. I was in hospital in Brussels and then put on to a train, which took me to a hospital near Le Touquet. I remember writing home to my guardian uncle saying that we'd had a go at the Boche and that the Boche had had a go at me and that I was in a hospital miles behind the line – as I thought. But the Germans entered that place the next day and the hospital was evacuated and I was taken on a hospital ship to Southampton.

I was in hospital for about a month after that and then rejoined the battalion, which by that time was reforming at Bridlington on the coast. I rejoined having no idea about the VC until August. It took some time, you see. I think they had to get witnesses and so forth. I don't really know how they work it.

Sergeant Major Martin McLane, 2nd Battalion, Durham Light Infantry:

One day I was drilling the men in a yard called Marshall's Yard, which opens out on the main road from Bridlington to Hull, and I spotted Lieutenant Annand. I had a lot of time for this officer. He had been wounded and I didn't know he was back with the battalion, and he's standing across the road so I halt the men, tell them they could smoke and I go across and salute him and say, 'Hello, sir. How are you? You got over your wounds all right?' And he got on chatting with us and I said, 'What are you doing here anyway?' If you can imagine a long high wall, like they have round the royalty's estates: he was standing with his back against the wall and there was a farmhouse further along [where the battalion had its headquarters].

And I got on chatting with him and he says, 'Well, sergeant-major, you might be pleased to know I've been sent here to wait for the news reporters.' I said, 'What for?' He says, 'I've been awarded the Victoria Cross.'

Now that's the first we knew about it, that he'd been put in for an award, and I was delighted for him. I said, 'Well, what are you standing here for, sir?' He says, 'They've had me in to headquarters and told me that I'm due for a VC, that the reporters are coming to meet me and that I should wait outside.' I said, 'They never sat you down and gave you a cup of coffee or tea or made you at home?' He said, 'No.' He was standing on his own outside! So I got the men around and told them about him, a lot of them knew him, and they were delighted to know he'd got the VC. But for a man who'd really fought and made history for the regiment, which everybody's so proud of now, to be left standing on his own in a lone country road with no traffic passing, just on his own till we went over and spoke to him …

BARTON, Cyril Joe

Rank/Service: Pilot Officer, 578 Squadron, RAF Volunteer Reserve
VC Location: RAF Museum, Hendon
Date of Gazette: 27 June 1944
Place/Date or Birth: Elveden, Suffolk, 5 June 1921
Place/Date or Death: Ryhope, Co. Durham, 31 March 1944
Grave: Bonner Hill Road Cemetery, Kingston-upon-Thames, Surrey
Memorials: Kingston-upon-Thames Cemetery; War Memorial, Ryhope
Town/County Connections: Elveden, Suffolk; New Malden, Surrey

Account of Deed: On the night of 30 March 1944, Pilot Officer Barton (168669) was captain and pilot of a Halifax aircraft detailed to attack Nurenberg. When some 70 miles short of the target, the aircraft was attacked by a Junkers 88. The burst of fire from the enemy made the inter-communication system useless. One engine was damaged when a Messerschmitt 210 joined in the fight. The bomber's machine-guns were out of action and the gunners were unable to return the fire.

Fighters continued to attack the aircraft as it approached the target area and, in the confusion caused by the failure of the communications system at the height of the battle, a signal was misinterpreted and the navigator, air bomber and wireless operator left the aircraft by parachute.

Pilot Officer Barton faced a situation of dire peril. His aircraft was damaged, his navigational team had gone and he could not communicate with the remainder of the crew. If he continued his mission, he would be at the mercy of hostile fighters when silhouetted against the fires in the target area, and if he survived he would have to make a 4½ hour journey home on three engines across heavily defended territory. Determined to press home his attack at all costs, he flew on and, reaching the target, released the bombs himself.

As Pilot Officer Barton turned for home the propeller of the damaged engine, which was vibrating badly, flew off. It was also discovered that two of the petrol tanks had suffered damage and were leaking. Pilot Officer Barton held to his course and, without navigational aids and in spite of strong head-winds, successfully avoided the most dangerous defence areas on his route. Eventually he crossed the English coast only 90 miles north of his base.

By this time the petrol supply was nearly exhausted. Before a suitable landing place could be found, the port engine stopped. The aircraft was now too low to be abandoned successfully. Pilot Officer Barton therefore ordered the three remaining members of his crew to take up their crash stations. Then, with only one engine working, he made a gallant attempt to land clear of the houses over which he was flying. The aircraft finally crashed and Pilot Officer Barton lost his life, but his three comrades survived.

Pilot Officer Barton had previously taken part in four attacks on Berlin and fourteen other operational missions. On one of these two members of his crew were wounded during a determined effort to locate the target despite the appalling weather conditions.

In gallantly completing his last mission in the face of almost impossible odds, this officer displayed unsurpassed courage and devotion to duty.

Biographical Detail: Cyril Joe Barton was the son of Frederick J Barton and Ethel Barton, of New Malden. During his youth he was a Boy Scout with the 1st Oxsott Scout group (Surrey). He volunteered for aircrew duties and joined the Royal Air Force Volunteer Reserve RAFVR on 16 April 1941, qualifying as a Sergeant Pilot 10 November 1942. He then trained at No. 1663 Heavy Conversion Unit at Rufforth, Yorkshire. On 5 September 1943, Barton and his crew joined No. 78 squadron and Barton was commissioned as a Pilot Officer three weeks later. Undertaking their first operational sortie against Montlucon, Barton completed nine sorties with No. 78 squadron before 15 January 1944, and was then posted to No. 578 Squadron at Burn in North Yorkshire. Their second sortie with the new squadron was to Stuttgart in Halifax LK797 (codename LK-E). By 30 March 1944, they had completed six sorties in LK797 – which the crew had named 'Excalibur'.

Barton Green in New Malden, Surrey, where he had attended Beverley Boys School, was named in his honour during the early 1950s and Barton Road at the Yorkshire Air Museum in Elvington, North Yorkshire, was named in his honour, on the forty-sixth anniversary of his death. A housing estate in Ryhope, Barton Park, was also named after him, while a nearby street was named Halifax Place, after the bomber he flew. Kingston College which Barton attended, also offers an annual prize for the student of the year which is named after him. A painting in his memory hangs in the Wheatsheaf public house at Burn, North Yorkshire, where 578 Squadron was once based.

BRADFORD, George Nicholson
Rank/Service: Lieutenant Commander, Royal Navy
VC Location: Lord Ashcroft VC Collection
Date of Gazette: 17 March 1919
Place/Date of Birth: Darlington, Co. Durham, 23 April 1887
Place/Date of Death: Zeebrugge, Belgium, 23 April 1918
Memorials: Blankenberge Communal Cemetery, Belgium
Town/County Connections: Darlington, Co. Durham

Significant Remarks: Brother of Lieutenant Colonel R B Bradford, VC.

Account of Deed: On the night of 22/23 April 1918 at Zeebrugge, Belgium, Lieut-Commander George Nicholson Bradford was in command of the naval storming parties embarked in *Iris II*. When *Iris II* proceeded alongside the mole great difficulty was experienced in placing the parapet-anchors owing to the motion of the ship. An attempt was made to land by the scaling-ladders before the ship was secured. Lieutenant Claude E K Hawkins managed to get one ladder in position and actually reached the parapet, the ladder being crushed to pieces just as he stepped off it. This very gallant young officer was last seen defending himself with his revolver. He was killed on the parapet.

Although securing the ship was not a part of his duties, Lieutenant-Commander Bradford climbed up the derrick which carried a large parapet-anchor and was rigged out over the port side. During the climb the ship was surging up and down and the derrick crashing on the mole. Awaiting his opportunity he jumped with the parapet-anchor on to the mole and placed it in position. Immediately after hooking on the parapet-anchor, Lieutenant-Commander Bradford was riddled with bullets from machine-guns and fell into the sea between the mole and the ship. Attempts to recover his body failed.

Lieutenant-Commander Bradford's action was one of absolute self-sacrifice. Without a moment's hesitation he went to certain death, recognising that in such an action lay the only possible chance of securing *Iris II* and enabling her storming parties to land.

Biographical Detail: Some families seem to breed medal-winners. Whether acts of extreme bravery are sparked by a particular gene, or provoked by a spirit of competition between brothers, there are many striking instances of VCs, DSOs and MCs being won by members of the same family. However, in this respect no record is more remarkable in either World War than that of the Bradford brothers who came to be known as 'the Fighting Bradfords' – Thomas (1886–1966), George (1887–1918), James (1889–1917) and Roland (1892–1917) – who between them created the astonishing record of winning two VCs, a DSO, two MCs and three mentions in despatches during the First World War.[2]

A harsh upbringing undoubtedly moulded the character of the four Bradford boys – their father George was a rough, tough manager of collieries in County Durham, who frequently beat, cuffed and kicked his sons, believing that corporal punishment was not only a valuable corrective when they misbehaved, but also a beneficial influence in the general development of character. His uncompromising regime had the effect, which he probably intended, of teaching the boys to control themselves: he taught them never to succumb to fear or pain, and thus helped make them all outstanding leaders.

Their mother, Amy, was entirely different. A gentle, timid woman from Willesborough in Kent, as disorganised as she was attractive, she lived in dread of her thuggish husband, who criticised her sarcastically for failing to maintain the standards of housekeeping which he thought were his due. Getting little comfort from him, she bestowed her love on her children. Yet in a curious way she, too, prepared them to become fighters, for she fired their imagination by reading aloud stories of war and adventure in which patriotic heroes always triumphed, and classics such as *Tom Brown's Schooldays*. Among their favourites was Macaulay's epic poem *Lays of Ancient Rome*, and in particular the story of: 'how well Horatius kept the bridge in the brave days of old'.

In the garden they often acted out the sagas which excited them, taking sides to recreate battles in far-flung corners of the British Empire, and struggles in which clean-cut English soldiers invariably overcame the heathen.

They were of good Border stock, and for their first few years their home was Carrwood House, a substantial dwelling that stood on its own among green fields outside the village of Witton Park, 3 miles south-west of Bishop Auckland. Then in 1894 the family moved to Morton Palms Farm, near Darlington, where the healthy outdoor life helped all the brothers grow up fit and strong.

Thomas (aged 8) and George (7) walked to and from the Primary Department of the Queen Elizabeth Grammar School in Darlington – 4 miles there and 4 miles back. Luckily for them, and for the peace of the household in general, their father was often away on business; but one of the few positive contributions he made to their development was to encourage them in sporting activities: cricket, rugby and above all boxing. It was presumably their mother who inculcated a strong religious faith, and a habit of regular attendance at church.

In 1898 the family moved to Milbank House, in Darlington itself, and there it was augmented by the arrival of a daughter, Amy, born in 1901. Sometimes known as 'Ginger', she became very close to her brothers, and frequently corresponded with them when they went to war. As the boys left home, one by one, they escaped their father's influence to a great extent, and he died in 1911, aged 66, before any of them had won a medal.

After schools in Darlington, George the second son went, in 1901, at the age of 14, to the Royal Naval College at Eltham, in south-east London, and Eastman's School, in Southsea, near Portsmouth, where he remained until he joined the Royal Navy in 1902 as an officer cadet on board HMS *Britannia*. Like his brothers, he was athletic and good at sports, cricket and rugby among them; but his main love was boxing, at which he became highly skilled – winner of numerous prizes, and welterweight champion of the Navy. Even during the war years he fought in many tournaments and exhibition bouts organised between ships.

Maybe boxing was the means whereby he worked off his aggression. Out of the ring he seems to have been a cheerful, easy going fellow, much liked by his contemporaries, who saw him as the best sort of English gentleman. He was particularly fond of his young sister Amy, to whom he wrote jokey letters:

> You are quite right about the canoe, the stern is the place to steer from – only great men like me can do it from forward. I suppose you like David Copperfield. Dombey & Son is one of my favourites ... The enclosed is a somewhat fantastic crest. The animal is actually a flea. It strikes one as rather heavily misplaced wit ... Mother sent me the book Whyte Melville, what I wanted was the song though I stupidly did not say so. Good luck to you at school, keep the Bradford name like that of Bayard chevalier sans peur – possibly misquoted but conveys the right idea.

He also wrote loving letters to his mother, particularly at times when he knew she was ill or distressed (even to her he always signed himself formally G. N. Bradford – never 'George'). Other members of the family attributed his affectionate, relaxed attitude to the fact that, leaving home at 14, he escaped his father's baleful influence earlier than his brothers, and so was less inclined to see people and events in terms of black and white.

One of his most attractive characteristics was his optimism. Wherever he happened to be, he felt sure that the war was going well. 'I think the allies have never been in [a] stronger position than now and am very confident in the result,' he wrote to Amy in February 1917. When James died of wounds on 14 May, he told her, 'You should give your mother an optimistic letter from time to time. She has been much shaken by her illness and by [losing] Jimmy.' Then he immediately went on to say, 'Weather here glorious, winning the war, in fact everything going splendidly. No aches, no pains, a pleasure to be alive.'

Until its very last moments, when suddenly his courage blazed up in glory, his naval career was worthy but undistinguished. Nevertheless, there was one incident which gave a good indication of his mettle. In 1909 he was serving as a sub-lieutenant on the destroyer HMS *Chelmer* when she and her sister destroyer HMS *Doon* were ordered to Dover to collect King George V and ferry him to Calais for an official visit. At 03.20 on the morning of 3 March the *Doon*, steaming at 15 knots, collided in mid-Channel with a trawler, the *Halcyon*, slicing open her port side. Under George's command, the *Chelmer's* whaler was launched and went to rescue the trawler's crew. In about fifteen minutes the open rowing boat had taken three men aboard, and it had pulled away when a signal came from the *Doon* saying that there was a fourth member of the crew – a boy who had fallen into the hold. With the *Halcyon* about to sink, the whaler pulled back to the stricken vessel: George jumped aboard and vanished into the black cavern of the hold, reappearing with the unconscious boy in his arms. Scarcely had he regained the whaler when the *Halcyon* up-ended, with only her bow above the surface, and then sank. His courage, physical fitness and decisiveness were noticed by senior officers, and on 30 July, as a reward for his gallant rescue, he was promoted to full lieutenant.

He served throughout the First World War in the battleship *Orion*, and was present at the great battle of Jutland – the titanic yet inconclusive clash between the British and German fleets on 31 May 1916; no records of his conduct survive, but he must have proved an efficient officer, for, as he informed Amy in a letter dated 5 August 1917:

> *Moi*, I am a Lieutenant Commander, having completed eight years as Lieutenant, and as the designing mothers of Portsmouth would say, 'He gets another shilling a day now.'

Then, on the 23 April 1918, came the naval raid on the port of Zeebrugge, in Belgium, which made his name. For months the Admiralty had been gravely worried by the strength of the German naval presence at Zeebrugge, which stands at the seaward end of a 6-mile canal leading inland to the harbour at Bruges. Enemy warships based there, and submarines in particular, were posing a severe threat to Allied shipping: attempts had been made to put Zeebrugge out of action by heavy naval bombardments, but the port's defences were extremely strong, and by the end of 1917 it had become clear that only drastic action would bottle up the ships using the base.

A complex raid was planned, chiefly by Vice-Admiral Roger Keyes (later Admiral of the Fleet, Lord Keyes). The principal objective was to sail three block-ships into the harbour and sink them in the mouth of the canal, so as to seal access to the English Channel. The British crews were all volunteers, highly trained and ready for the fight, who nonetheless knew they were unlikely to survive the firestorm from the German batteries.

To give them a chance of getting past the guns on the mole, an infantry force would launch a diversionary attack to distract the defenders, and at the same time two submarines loaded with high explosive would ram the pillars of the viaduct which formed part of the mole and blow a gap in it, thus preventing any reinforcements coming up to the critical area.

In the end it proved to be the ultimate example of heroic failure. The Germans quickly removed the obstructions, and the U-boats continued to operate throughout the summer – but in that one brief morning, eleven men won the VC, twenty-one the DSO, twenty-nine the DSC, among many other awards. Among the dead was George who perished in an heroic attempt to attach a grappling iron: he was shot and fell between two warships.

His body was washed up 5 miles down the coast to the west, a few days later, and he was buried with full military honours by the Germans in the town's communal cemetery. His extraordinary heroism was at first acknowledged only by a mention in despatches, but on 23 February 1919 Vice-Admiral Keyes recommended him for a Victoria Cross, and in his letter to the Admiralty wrote:

Lieutenant Commander Bradford's action was one of absolute self-sacrifice; without a moment's hesitation he went to certain death, recognising that in such action lay the only possible chance of securing *Iris II* and enabling her storming parties to land.

On 14 March Keyes wrote to Mrs Bradford:

> You may hear before my letter reaches you that your very gallant son George has been awarded the posthumous Victoria Cross which he so heroically earned on his birthday. I knew he would eventually get it, because although many actions were performed on that night by officers and men who survived, and by others who gave their lives, amongst the latter your son's act of glorious self-sacrifice stood out, I thought, alone …
>
> I know how deeply you have suffered in this war, but to have been the mother of such splendid sons must have been some consolation to you.

News of George's award appeared in the *London Gazette* on 17 March 1919. Initially, five other officers and men who took part in the raid had won VCs, but after reconsideration, another was awarded to Lieutenant Commander Arthur Harrison, who led HMS *Vindictive's* assault parties on to the mole. Petty Officer Hallihan, who dived into the sea trying to rescue George, received a posthumous mention in despatches.

The tributes sent in by other officers were of quite exceptional warmth and sincerity. Admiral the Lord Jellicoe declared that he had 'admired his [George's] character as well as his great personal ability … He died, as one would have expected him to die, under circumstances of the greatest gallantry and supreme sacrifice.' Captain Fullerton, who had commanded HMS *Orion*, wrote to his mother: 'I can truly say a more honourable, straight and gallant English gentleman never lived … he was loved by all', and the *Orion's* chaplain added: 'He was so magnificent, so firm and patient and kind that we all, both officers and men, looked to him for guidance and advice.'

When Captain Carpenter, who commanded the *Vindictive*, began to give lectures about the raid, people kept asking him to put the whole story into a book, and he did just that. *The Blocking of Zeebrugge* was published in 1922, and brought the hazards of the operation vividly to life; but in a letter to

George's mother, Amy, the author confessed that he had found it extremely difficult to do him justice;

> because my enthusiasm concerning his gallantry cannot be measured by mere words. His death was a terrible blow to us all. We feel, however, that we should be better men for having known him. He was a great gentleman and loved by all with whom he was associated, and his name will go down in history and act as a spur to the coming generations whose emotions will be bestirred deeply whenever his splendid deed is mentioned.

Such plaudits, and the fact that the family had won its second VC, may have given poor Amy some comfort. But the loss of a third son within the year[5] overwhelmed her: she became fairly eccentric, and went to live for the rest of her days with her two sisters in Kent.

Mrs Bradford received George's posthumous VC from King George V on 3 April 1919 at Buckingham Palace. It was the second time she had attended such a ceremony on behalf of one of her sons. Hardly ever speaking of her sons, as if she wanted to forget the past, nevertheless she appeared at every Remembrance Day ceremony in Folkestone wearing two Victoria Crosses and one Military Cross. She also placed 'In Memoriam' notices in *The Times* on the anniversaries of her three sons' deaths every year until her own demise in 1951 aged 91.

BRADFORD, Roland Boyes

Rank/Service: Lieut-Col. (later Brigadier General) Comd., 9th Bn, DLI
Other Decorations: MC
VC Location: Durham Light Infantry Museum, Durham
Date of Gazette: 25 November 1916
Place/Date of Birth: Etherley, Co. Durham, 22 February 1892
Place/Date of Death: Cambrai, France, 30 November 1917
Memorials: Hermies British Cemetery, France
Town/County Connections: Darlington, Co. Durham

Significant Remarks: At the time of his death, he was the youngest Brigadier General in the British army and was the brother of Lt-Cdr G N Bradford VC.

Account of Deed: On 1 October 1916 at Eaucourt L'Abbaye, France, when a leading battalion had suffered very severe casualties and the commander was wounded, its flank was dangerously exposed to the enemy. At the request of the wounded commander, Lieutenant Colonel Bradford took command of that battalion in addition to his own. By his fearless energy under fire of all descriptions, and skilful leadership of both battalions, he succeeded in rallying the attack and capturing and defending the objective.

Biographical Detail: Roland was the youngest of the four brothers, and by far the liveliest, endowed with an excellent mind and an ebullient sense of fun. His sister Amy remembered him as 'a tremendous tease', who used to invent lurid crimes that her dolls had committed and then sentence them to death, either having them hanged or chopping off their heads (but generally replacing casualties). He grew up a complex character, simultaneously full of imagination and yet excessively casual. He resented the fact that he was the junior member of the family, and (according to his brother Thomas) 'disliked being suppressed on account of his youth'. The result was that he argued energetically with his elders, always determined to make his point – and yet he did not often annoy them, for he was blessed with a great deal of natural charm.

Although intelligent, he had little interest in most academic subjects, and after various schools in Darlington he went on to Epsom College in Surrey, but left prematurely in 1909 without matriculating. Yet he loved language and literature, both English and French, and spent countless hours learning poems which he would recite by heart to the family or to himself. As a boy of 14 he compiled a notebook in which he kept meticulous records of his tame pigeons. Admiring them greatly, he was upset when the cat got one of their squabs, and at the end of the year he quoted from *Antony and Cleopatra*:

The following lines of Shakespeare are worthy of the hen:

> Age cannot wither her, nor custom stale
> Her infinite variety.
> Total at close of season, eight eggs. Two birds lived …

His passion was physical exercise. Not only did he excel at rugby, winning his First XV colours at Epsom, and playing cricket and hockey, he also boxed and hunted, and wrote instructional pamphlets on how to keep fit, among them 'Neck Exercises' and 'Trunk Bending'. 'It is quite common to see a well-developed body attached to the head by a thin and weedy neck,' he wrote: 'A bull neck is still more unsightly, but a neck obtained by physical exercise is shapely and handsome. As the neck gets very little freedom, being encased in a stiff collar during the day, I think it of special importance that it should receive exercise.'

Having left school at 17, he had no clear ideas about a career, and for a few months he drifted aimlessly; but at Epsom he had much enjoyed the activities of the college Cadet Corps, and it was no surprise to the family when, in 1910, he joined the 5th Battalion of the Durham Light Infantry (Territorial Force). After two summer camps, in 1910 and 1911, he attended a month's course at Colchester, and this, it seems, persuaded him to aim for the regular army. Having joined the Special Reserve, he went to a military crammer in London, worked hard there through the winter, and in March

1912 passed the examination for a commission – which enabled him to join the 2nd Battalion of the DLI as a 2nd lieutenant.

From the start senior officers were aware that they had recruited a subaltern with a strong personality and exceptional gifts as a leader. As one of them put it, he was 'all keenness and enthusiasm in the right direction', with a streak of originality and a strong sense of humour thrown in. He was never a teetotaller, but drank sparingly, smoked very little and spent much time trying to develop minor inventions. One of these was an aluminium body-shield, light enough to be carried into battle by an infantry soldier. It seemed a good idea, but Roland was disappointed to find that on the range rifle bullets easily penetrated the metal.

The outbreak of war in August 1914 found the 2nd Battalion at its annual camp in Wales, but within three days it was on the move, and by 20 September it was on the right of the British front line in France, on the ridge north of Troyon. Roland by then had become one of D Company's platoon commanders, and nobody can have had a more ferocious baptism of fire. In bitter fighting, the Durhams found themselves enfiladed (fired on from the side) by Germans who had broken through on their flank, and even though in the end they drove the enemy back, their casualties were appalling. D Company alone lost five officers and thirty-six other ranks dead, besides six officers and ninety-two other ranks wounded. Among those killed was the company commander, Major Robb, and Roland was the only officer to survive unscathed.

He again became involved in heavy fighting at the end of October, when attacks and counter-attacks continued almost without a break for several days. On 28 October his platoon was manning a road barricade when enemy troops began to outflank them in an attempt at encirclement, and he held the position until the last possible moment, with a tenacity never forgotten by an unnamed NCO, who wrote the following morning:

We had another big do at Bois Grenier, and Lieutenant R. B. Bradford proved at this period one of the finest officers I have ever had the pleasure of being with. We fought continually for two days and nights, but on the third night we were almost surrounded, and he gave me orders to watch the main road to Lille with three men; and when I gave my report to him, he brought us out, and it was owing to his skill and valour that we got safely through.

As a result of this action, Roland received a mention in despatches 'for gallant and distinguished services in the field'. This was published in the *London Gazette* of 17 February 1915, and on the following day the journal announced that he had won the newly created Military Cross, 'for services rendered in connection with operations in the field'.

The Durhams suffered further heavy casualties during that winter but again Roland came through unharmed. In March 1915 he was promoted to temporary captain, and on 3 May he was posted as adjutant to the 7th Battalion of the DLI, a territorial unit which had recently come out to France, and was commanded by Lieutenant Colonel E Vaux, of the brewing family. Two days later at a parade drawn up before General Sir John French, commander-in-chief of the British Expeditionary Force, an anonymous witness caught a revealing glimpse of him:

Captain Bradford MC stood in striking silhouette to those who noticed him, alongside our Colonel. A pleasanter smile no man could have seen than Lieutenant Bradford [wore] on that particular day, and he was among strangers of whom he could know nothing.

On paper the 7th Battalion was a pioneer unit, whose function was to build and repair trenches, excavate dugouts and so on; in practice, during the summer of 1915, it was often thrown into the front line. But between such crises, when things were relatively quiet, Roland found time for self-improvement, polishing his French, learning Spanish, taking elocution lessons by correspondence with a London teacher, and practising his public speaking by delivering words and gestures in front of a mirror.

By the end of the year many senior officers had discerned his outstanding qualities, and one promotion rapidly followed another. In December 1915 he moved to the 6th Battalion, DLI, again as adjutant; then in February 1916, after a spell of home leave, he became Brigade Major of 151 Brigade, and on 8 May he was transferred as second-in-command to the 9th Battalion, DLI, a territorial unit from Gateshead, with the rank of temporary major, still aged only 24. Colonel Vaux, his former commanding officer, wrote him a warm tribute:

> Our year together has been, in my opinion, a very wonderful one. Never since you joined me have you and I had a single wrong word, and honestly I feel deeply all the things you have done for me.

The 9th Battalion was the unit in which Roland made an indelible mark. As soon as he arrived he threw himself into the task of training, bringing all ranks up to a high standard of fitness. Yet he was also still involved in front-line patrolling, and on 15 June the *London Gazette* announced his second mention in despatches. Such was the impression he created that on 4 August he was promoted to acting lieutenant colonel and given command of the battalion.

On the Somme in July and August 1916, it had been Kitchener's New Army that had born the brunt of the fighting. In September, it was the turn of the Territorials. On 15 September, Temporary Lieutenant Colonel Bradford was wounded as he led the 9th battalion, DLI, as part of the 151st Brigade of the 50th Division, into battle for the first time against the German held trenches east of Martinpuich.

On 1 October, the 50th Division was ordered to capture Eaucourt l'Abbaye and the trenches east of Le Sars. The assault was timed for 3.15pm and was to be led on the right by the 6th Battalion DLI with 9th Battalion DLI close behind in support. As the Durhams waited in their trenches for the attack to begin, they came under heavy German artillery and machine-gun fire and Major Wilkinson, commanding 6th Battalion DLI, was badly wounded in the arm. As he was going back to the casualty clearing station, he met Roland Bradford and asked him to take command of his battalion.

Once permission had been given by Brigade Headquarters, Lieutenant Colonel Bradford rushed forward to the front line. Meanwhile, as the artillery barrage lifted from the German front line, the 6th battalion attacked Flers Line. They were on the extreme right of the 50th Division and immediately came under withering machine-gun fire, as the Division on their right had been unable to get into position on time. The attack ground to a halt, as men desperately sought cover in shell holes from the flying bullets. At that critical moment, Roland Bradford arrived. Ignoring the dangers, he immediately went amongst the soldiers, encouraging, organising and giving new, clear orders. For this action he was awarded the VC.

Though notification of the award of the Victoria Cross to Lieutenant (Temporary Lieutenant Colonel) Roland Boys Bradford appeared in the *London Gazette* on 25 November 1916 – 'For most conspicuous bravery and good leadership in attack' – he was too busy to go home; he had a battalion to run.

Roland was finally presented with his Victoria Cross by King George V during an open-air ceremony in Hyde Park on 2 June 1917.

Two incidents demonstrate the quiet and unassuming character of Roland Bradford. After winning the Victoria Cross, Roland on a period of leave visited his home town of Darlington, the mayor asked him if he might arrange a public welcome. Roland's response was that if anything of the sort were done he would get straight into a train and return to London. No discourtesy was intended, but whatever personal ambition Roland had ever had was entirely obliterated by his love for and pride in his men. The honour conferred upon him was an honour to his battalion even more than to himself.

Roland also used his time on leave in 1916 to canvass the corridors of Whitehall on behalf of his men. His objective was that the troops be given the same privileges of home leave granted to the officers. In his determination to guard the interests of his men, there is some conclusive evidence that, on this subject of leave, Roland did not mince his words when speaking to those of higher rank than himself. He was always thinking about his men and urging that more of them should be sent on leave. Apparently things reached something of a crisis on one occasion when a General paid a visit to the 9th Battalion of the Durham Light Infantry which Roland commanded. Without any hesitation, Roland tackled the General upon the subject of leave, and during the conversation he frankly stated that the leave which ought to go to the fighting troops was being 'taken by the staff behind the lines'.

This remark not unnaturally caused the subsequent conversation to be more than a little animated. It was written of this incident that 'For a little time the General eyed Bradford up and down as though he would place him under arrest and then told him that leave for the men was his first consideration, and that the leave was properly allotted.' It is said, however, that Roland refused to be convinced, and that it was perhaps fortunate for him that the man with whom he was dealing had a considerable knowledge of human nature as well as some sense of humour. The incident ended with the General patting Roland on the back and remarking that he was damned glad someone was as interested in the men's leave as he himself was.

Contemporaries bore witness to his exceptional ability and character: they described his magnetism, his efficiency, his dedication to training, his capacity for giving clear orders, his skill as a tactician, his attention to detail, his personal courage – all of which made him an outstanding leader. Also, as one fellow officer, Major E H Veitch, recorded:

> He had an extraordinarily charming personality. His smile and greeting on meeting you actually made you feel that there was nothing he liked better than to see you. His first thought for everyone, officers and men, was their comfort. His attention to details was extraordinary. He saw to everything himself, even to superintending a working party.

Yet he was also a strict disciplinarian, who insisted that his men shaved every day, even if they were in the line, and kept their trenches free of rubbish. When he realised how many of them suffered from skin disease – often exacerbated or brought on by lice – he took the advice of the regimental medical officer and decreed that they should sunbathe naked for an hour every day. The order produced unfortunate repercussions, for some of Roland's colleagues thought it odd that he should enjoy the sight of young men's bodies: they had already remarked on how little interest he showed in girls, and some even said that he hated women in general. Now word went round that he was homosexual. The rumours seem to have been unfounded: it was true that he sometimes appeared unsociable, preferring his own company to that of his fellow officers, and withdrawing to his tent, where he would practise his public speaking or pray; but there is no evidence of homosexual inclinations – and in any case, the order to sunbathe merely specified that the men should take their shirts off.

On his return to the front line in the following month, one evening in July 1917, whilst in reserve resting after the Battle of Arras, Roland Bradford ordered the 9th Battalion on parade. He then told the assembled soldiers: 'I want you to sing the hymn the band will now play, every night at retreat, whether you are in the trenches or in billets.' The band then struck up the song *Abide with Me*. This became the battalion's hymn and was soon adopted by the entire regiment, and is still the regimental hymn today. As a postscript to this incident, in December 1917, just a few weeks after the death of Roland, the 9th Battalion DLI left the horrors of the Ypres Salient and moved into billets. That night, after *Last Post* was sounded, came the hymn *Abide with Me*. A soldier newly arrived in the Battalion sneered: 'What's this? A bloody Sunday School!' He was immediately punched to the ground by Private Bobby Davidson, a veteran soldier wearing the ribbon of the Military Medal, who told him: 'That hymn was taught to us by a better bloody soldier than you will ever be.'

On 10 November 1917, Bradford was given command of the 186th Brigade of the 62nd (West Riding) Division and, reluctantly, left the 9th Battalion. Sadly, the career of Brigadier General Roland Boys Bradford VC MC lasted just twenty days. During the Battle of Cambrai on 30 November 1917, he was killed by a stray German shell near his Brigade Headquarters in Bourlon Wood and was buried in Hermies British Cemetery. When he died, aged 25 years old, he was the youngest Brigadier General in the British Army.

For many years after the war Mrs Amy Bradford attended the annual Armistice Day service at the War Memorial in Folkestone, Kent. Like so many other grieving mothers, she wore the medals of her children killed in the Great War. She had lost three of her four sons, but, like no other mother, she wore two Victoria Crosses, in memory of George and Roland, who were the only brothers to gain the Victoria Cross during the First World War.

COLLIN, Joseph Henry
Rank/Service: 2nd Lieut, 1/4Bn King's Own Royal (Lancaster) Regiment
VC Location: King's Own Royal (Lancaster) Regiment Museum, Lancaster
Date of Gazette: 25 June 1915
Place/Date of Birth: Jarrow, Co. Durham, 11 April 1893
Place/Date of Death: Givenchy, France, 9 April 1918
Grave: Vieille-Chapelle New Military Cemetery, France
Memorials: Palmer Hospital, Jarrow
Town/County Connections: Jarrow, Co. Durham

Account of Deed: After offering a long and gallant resistance against heavy odds in Orchard Keep held by his platoon, this officer, with only five of his men remaining, slowly withdrew in the face of superior numbers, contesting every inch of the ground. The enemy were pressing him hard with bombs and machine-gun fire from close range. Single-handed 2nd Lieutenant Collin attacked the machine-gun team. After firing his revolver into the enemy, he seized a Mills grenade and threw it into the hostile team, putting the gun out of action, killing four of the team and wounding two others. Observing a second hostile machine-gun firing, he took a Lewis gun, and selecting a high point of vantage on the parapet whence he could engage the gun, he, unaided, kept the enemy at bay until he fell mortally wounded.

Biographical Detail: Joseph Henry Collin was born to Mary and Joseph Collin of 8 Patterill Terrace, Harraby Castle, on 11 April 1893 in Jarrow, Co. Durham and was baptised at St Bed's church, Jarrow. Later the family moved to Carlisle, where Joseph was educated at St Patrick's School. At the outbreak of war he was working at Hepworth's in Carlisle, but in 1915 he enlisted in the Argyll & Sutherland Highlanders with whom he served in France, being promoted to Sergeant. Selected for a commission, he was posted in October 1917 as a 2nd Lieutenant to the 1/4th Battalion King's Own in France.

2nd Lieutenant Collin was originally buried in the King's Liverpool graveyard in Cuinchy, but was later relocated to Vieille Chapelle British

Military Cemetery. Every year Carlisle schools compete for the 'Collin Shield', a trophy for a mile race presented in his memory by his family. His Victoria Cross was presented to the King's Own Royal Regiment Museum by his family in 1956. In this century his bronze memorial plaque came up for auction in Carlisle, and thanks to the generosity of the public and a grant from the MLA/V&A Museum the Regiment was able to beat off three other bidders to secure the plaque at a cost of £2,500.

COOPER, Edward

Rank/Service: Sergeant (later Major), 12th Engineers, King's Royal Rifle Corps
Other Decorations: Medaille Militaire (France)
VC Location: Green Dragon Museum, Stockton
Date of Gazette: 14 September 1917
Place/Date of Birth: Stockton-on-Tees, Co. Durham, 4 May 1896
Place/Date of Death: Stockton-on-Tees, 19 August 1985
Grave: Teesside Crematorium, Middlesbrough
Memorials: Stockton-on-Tees Public Library
Town/County Connections: Stockton-on-Tees

Account of Deed: On 16 August 1917 at Langemarck, Belgium, enemy machine-guns from a concrete blockhouse 250 yards away were holding up the advance of the battalion on the left and also causing heavy casualties to Sergeant Cooper's own battalion. With four men he rushed towards the blockhouse, but although they fired at the garrison at very close range (100 yards) the machine-guns were not silenced, as a consequence Sergeant Cooper ran straight at them and fired his revolver into an opening in the blockhouse; the machine-guns ceased firing and the garrison surrendered. Seven machine-guns and forty-five prisoners were captured.

Biographical Detail: Sergeant Edward Cooper was not sent on leave until 15 January 1918, nearly five months after the action in front of Langemarck, and when he left the front he still did not know anything about an award. It was not until he was sitting in a YMCA café at King's Cross railway station that he happened to see a newspaper carrying a list of the new VCs. The name of Chavasse caught his eye, Captain Noel Chavasse who had just won a Bar to his VC, one of only three men ever to do so and the poor man died shortly afterwards. Next in alphabetical order was 'Cooper. E.' It was not until he had read and reread the name and the regimental number that he realised that it was his own citation that he was reading. The small shy sergeant in the corner of the carriage said nothing, but when the train finally reached Darlington, where he had to change, Cooper was astonished to find his father and his elder brother waiting for him. Then, to his enormous embarrassment, a civic reception awaited him at Stockton-on-Tees.

For thirty-five years he lived in modest obscurity until the Victoria Cross Association was formed in 1953 and someone hunted him down. Suddenly he was a hero all over again. On 24 July 1985 Edward Cooper VC was given the Freedom of Stockton but he died less than four weeks later on 19 August 1985.

> The Stockton-on-Tees Lodge of Unity is proud of all its Brethren past and present but it is hard to not to single out Bro. Edward Cooper V.C. for a special mention. As the first recipient of the highest order of Gallantry in Stockton we are proud to be associated with Bro. Edward who was a proud Freemason. Bro. Edward is still remembered at the Lodge as the Square and Compass that he presented to the Lodge are still used every meeting. It is also worth mentioning out of interest that the research of W. Bro. Granville Angell has shown over 10% of Victoria Crosses awarded were to Free-masons.

On Thursday 16 September 2010 an interesting lot came up for auction comprising: Major Cooper's KRRC Cap Badge worn in 1917, the Cap Badge of Sergeant William F. Burman VC (won during the Battle of Passchendaele on 20 September 1917) The Rifle Brigade. Also, a reproduction of a photograph showing the presentation by King George V of Cooper's VC and a transcript of the citation with a signed dedication in pen (to the vendor) from Major Cooper and reproduction of Private Tom Dresser VC. Excellent overall, all contained in bespoke presentation frames. Together with a framed photograph showing the vendor and Major Cooper at the presentation and plaque unveiling, Stockton-on-Tees, 16 August 1977.[6]

a poignant moment when, in error, Alfredo produced his Alien's Identity Card at the gate before fumbling in another pocket to find the King's official command!

During the ceremony, he confided to George VI about his internment at which the monarch promptly told him to forget about the POW camp and go straight home to the mining village of Easington Colliery. He did so and received a warm welcome from the local coal miners who had fought with the police at the start of the war to try and prevent his arrest.

Dennis is buried near Maastricht in the Netherlands while his brother Luigi also lies in a Commonwealth War Grave back home. In Durham City can be found 'Donnini Place' and a replica of Dennis's Victoria Cross is on display at Easington Colliery Workingmen's Club.

GOATE, William

Rank/Service: L-Corporal (later Corporal), 9th Lancers (Queen's Royal)
VC Location: 9/12th Royal Lancers Museum, Derby
Date of Gazette: 24 December 1858
Place/Date of Birth: Fritton, near Long Stratton, Norfolk, 12 January 1836
Place/Date of Death: Southsea, Hants, 26 October 1901
Grave: Highland Road Cemetery, Portsmouth (erected 2003)
Town/County Connections: Norwich; Jarrow, Co. Durham

Account of Deed: On 6 March 1858 at Lucknow, India, Lance-Corporal Goate dismounted in the presence of the enemy in order to take up the body of a major, which he then attempted to take off the field, but was forced to relinquish the act as he was surrounded by hostile cavalry. He did not, however, give up, but went a second time under heavy fire and recovered the body.

Biographical Detail: William Goate was born 12 January 1836 in the Norfolk village of Fritton to the south of Norwich. His father, a farmer, died when William was only 5 years old, leaving a widow and eleven children to manage the farm. Life was very hard, and all the family had to work long hours in the fields. When William was big enough, he was entrusted with looking after the horses, which served him well in the next phase of his life.

Tiring of the grind of the family farm and the stultifying life of the village, William left home and travelled the dozen or so miles into Norwich, where his experience with horses secured him a job as a groom. When he was 18, he decided he wanted another change and went to London and joined the Army. It is not clear whether it was a first choice or because he was unable to find work, and William was seduced by the tales of adventure told by the recruiting sergeants who plied their trade around Westminster.

On 21 November 1853, William enlisted in the 9th Lancers and spent the first nine months training at the cavalry depot at Maidstone. His service papers misspelled his name as 'Goat' and gave his occupation as 'labourer'.

On 21 July the following year, Goate embarked on the long gruelling sea voyage to join his regiment in India, which was achieved on 2 November.

A depiction of Queen Victoria presenting the Victoria Cross to some of the first recipients in Hyde Park, London, 26 June 1857. *(Royal Collection)*

VICTORIA CROSS-GALLERY.
Captain Bell, Royal Welsh Fusiliers, with the assistance of Private Syle, 7th Fusiliers, capturing a Russian Gun at the Battle of Alma. *(Crimea 1854.)*

B·B 2.

Captain Bell VC and Private Sykes VC capturing a Russian gun after the Battle of Alma (1854), from which are cast all the Victoria Cross medals.

Charles Anderson VC.

Captain Richard Annand VC and his wife at the
Durham Light Infantry Museum.

Somewhere in France, British soldiers rest and snatch a quick meal. (*TP5/3L photos*)

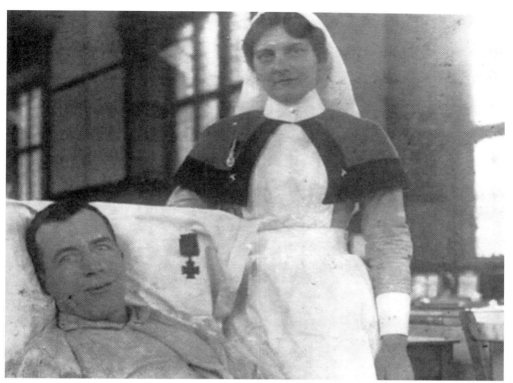

Lance Corporal Frederick Dobson VC in hospital with Nurse Grace Mitchell.

Many machine-gun battalions were manned by members of the Canadian Expeditionary Force (CEF): it was in such a battalion that Hugh Cairns VC fought.

Waiting to go ashore. D-Day, 6 June 1944.

Harry Christian receiving his VC medal from King George V while still recovering from wounds.

The British fleet in action at the Battle of Jutland.

Bren gun carriage moving up to the river Dyle line in Belgium, 10 May 1940.

Detail from Lady Butler's painting 'The Roll Call', showing the Grenadier Guards after the hard-fought Battle of Inkerman in which Lord Henry Percy fought and obtained a VC.

The gallant defence of Rorke's Drift, which formed the story of the iconic film *Zulu*.

Liddell at the control of a 'Boxkite' while learning to fly at the Vickers School, Brooklands.

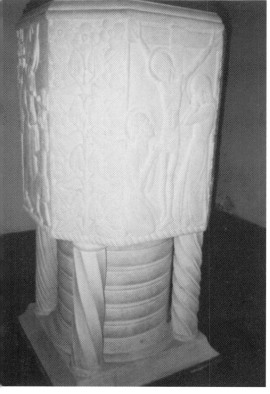

The font in the RC church of St Joseph, Pickering, designed by the renowned artist Eric Gill, which commemorates John Lydell VC (and was paid for by his father).

Frederick Corbett won his VC in August 1883 and is one of only eight who were stripped of their VC honour; Corbett lost his as a result of his conviction for embezzlement and theft from an officer.

Normandy, 1944: General Montgomery congratulates the men of the 50th Northumbrian division on their exploits on D-Day.

Thomas Kenny VC with his wife Isabel (née Applegarth). (*Photo courtesy of Joe Mulroy*)

Sergeant William McNally VC.

One of the many charges made by the 9th Lancers (Queen's Royal) during the taking of Lucknow.

The storming of one of the gates at Lucknow, India, March 1858.

Lieutenant G B McKean VC.

The reverse of the VC medal of George Chicken VC .

Bren gunner in the ruins of the monastery at Monte Cassino.

Crowds gather at the war memorial just south of Stockton-on-Tees parish church for the dedication ceremony on 31 May 1923 conducted by the Lord Bishop of Durham, Herbert Hensley Henson; the name of Thomas Young VC is inscribed on this memorial.

The inscriptions on the tomb of the Unknown Warrior, Westminster Abbey.

X X HIS LORD KNOWETH THEM THAT ARE HIS X X

BENEATH THIS STONE RESTS THE BODY
OF A BRITISH WARRIOR
UNKNOWN BY NAME OR RANK
BROUGHT FROM FRANCE TO LIE AMONG
THE MOST ILLUSTRIOUS OF THE LAND
AND BURIED HERE ON ARMISTICE DAY
11 NOV: 1920. IN THE PRESENCE OF
HIS MAJESTY KING GEORGE V
HIS MINISTERS OF STATE
THE CHIEFS OF HIS FORCES
AND A VAST CONCOURSE OF THE NATION

THUS ARE COMMEMORATED THE MANY
MULTITUDES WHO DURING THE GREAT
WAR OF 1914-1918 GAVE THE MOST THAT
MAN CAN GIVE LIFE ITSELF
FOR GOD
FOR KING AND COUNTRY
FOR LOVED ONES HOME AND EMPIRE
FOR THE SACRED CAUSE OF JUSTICE AND
THE FREEDOM OF THE WORLD

THEY BURIED HIM AMONG THE KINGS BECAUSE HE
HAD DONE GOOD TOWARD GOD AND TOWARD
HIS HOUSE

X X IN CHRIST SHALL ALL BE MADE ALIVE X X

GREATER LOVE HATH NO MAN THAN THIS

DYING AND BEHOLD WE LIVE

UNKNOWN AND YET WELL KNOWN

W & K London   THE UNKNOWN WARRIOR'S GRAVE IN WESTMINSTER ABBEY.
SHOWING THE AMERICAN CONGRESSIONAL MEDAL   No. 92

The tomb of the Unknown Warrior. Seventy-four VC holders made up the Guard of Honour at the interment in Westminster Abbey on Armistice Day 1920.

This was followed by another month-long trek across northern India to the cavalry station at Umballa (Amballa) on the Punjab border. The 9th Lancers had been stationed in India since 1842 and had been prominent in the Sikh Wars.

In an interview for *The Strand Magazine*,[7] William Goate recalled his service in India:

Well, after serving four years I was destined to ride in many a wild charge and see men and horses go down like ninepins, but I never thought of danger. When we got the order to charge, away we went determined to win, and I can tell you it must have been a terrible sight for any troops, let alone Sepoys, to see a regiment of cavalry sweeping down upon them.

Our fighting began in Delhi. We were at Umballa when the [Great] Mutiny broke out,[8] and we were ordered to join in the operations against Delhi. I was present at the siege and capture of that city. I will tell you of a little adventure of my own at this time.

Before the city was taken, I was on despatch duty at an advanced post with orders to fetch reinforcements when the enemy came out. One day I saw six men trying to steal round by the river into our camp. Believing them to be spies, I asked the officer in charge of the picket to allow me and two men to go and ascertain what their intentions were. He gave us leave.

We had a very difficult job to get down to the riverside on account of the rocks and; when we got up to the men, they showed fight. We shot three of them with our pistols – one each. Being on horseback, we then attacked them with the lance. One daring fellow struck at me and I couldn't get at him. He slightly wounded my horse and then made a run for the river. I jumped from my horse and, going into the water after him, ran him through with my lance. Meanwhile, the other two of my companions had settled the two remaining men. All the while, a heavy fire had played on us from the enemy's battery.

We now had to ride for our lives. On getting back to the camp, the officer in command sent me to the camp with a note to the Colonel of the regiment, who made me a lance-corporal then and there.

Goate continued:

the affair that I was in when I gained my Victoria Cross was before Lucknow, the second time. Early in 1858, the rebels had strongly fortified the place, and it became necessary for Sir Colin to take it. Our regiment had some hot work.

It was on 6 March that I won the Cross in action at Lucknow, having dismounted in the presence of the enemy and taken up the body of Major Percy Smith, 2nd Dragoon Guards, which I attempted to bring off the field; and after being obliged to relinquish it, being surrounded by the enemy's cavalry, going a second time, under a heavy fire, to recover the body, for which I received the Victoria Cross.

I will try to describe the fight, and what I saw of it. The enemy appeared in great force on the racecourse outside Lucknow, and the 9th Lancers, the 2nd Dragoon Guards and two native Cavalry Regiments were ordered to charge. The brigade swept on in grand style, and clashed into the enemy.

We had a fierce hand-to-hand fight; but our troops behaved splendidly, and at last, we broke them up. Then we were obliged to retire under a heavy fire. As we did so, Major Smith of the Dragoons, was shot through the body, and fell from his horse. Failing to catch him, I sprang to the ground; and; throwing the bridle-rein over my arm, raised the Major on to my shoulder; in this manner, I ran alongside my horse for some hundreds of yards, until I saw the enemy's cavalry close upon me. Clearly, I couldn't get away with my burden, so I determined to do what I could for myself.

Springing into my saddle, I shot the first Sepoy who charged; and with my empty pistol, felled another. This gave me the time to draw my sword; my lance having been left in the field. The Sepoys were now round me, cutting and hacking, but I managed to parry every slash and deliver many a fatal thrust. It was parry and thrust, thrust and parry all through, and I cannot tell you how many saddles I must have emptied the enemy didn't seem to know how to parry.

Taking advantage of this, I settled accounts with a jolly lot. I was determined not to be taken alive. At last, some Lancers saw me and came to my rescue. Thinking the Major might still be alive, I went again to rescue him, but it was not until the enemy's forces were driven back that we got his body.

After the action, General Sir Colin Campbell, General Sir Hope Grant and some of the cavalry officers shook hands with me and complimented me.

In regard to the sword and lance, I certainly prefer the lance; the lance is so keen, it goes through a man before he knows it. I was always very careful never to let a swordsman get under my lance, and in fighting with cavalry I made full use of the pennon to baffle an enemy's horse.

The weapons of troops on active service are made as keen as razors, and it was a common thing during the Mutiny to see a party of soldiers under the shade of a great tree waiting their turn to get their blades sharpened and the dints removed. Our gallant little army was like a ship cleaving its way through the sea, for wherever we went, the enemy, like the waters, closed in behind.

With the taking of Delhi, Cawnpore and Lucknow, the mutineers were in retreat. Goate and his comrades were constantly in the saddle as they pursued the dwindling numbers of mutineers across the plains of northern India. By the beginning of 1859, the Great Sepoy Mutiny was all but extinguished and the 9th Lancers were finally ordered back to England.

They embarked at the end of April and arrived home on 30 September, when they went into barracks at Exeter. As a reward for his arduous service, Goate was given thirty days furlough in November. In August 1860, the regiment marched from Exeter to take up station at Aldershot, where they remained until 1862. It was during 1860 that Goate attended an investiture at Windsor Castle and received his Victoria Cross from Queen Victoria.

Another move, to Brighton, lasted until the spring of 1864, when his final posting sent Goate to Dublin. On 22 November 1864, he was discharged as being medically unfit.[9]

William Goate, then aged 28, returned to his native Norfolk and lived for a while in Bungay. He married 18-year-old Sarah Ling and had a son, whom they named William. Work in rural East Anglia was becoming increasingly scarce as British agriculture declined towards the slump of the 1870s. Goate found work first as a railway porter, then as a warehouseman. Neither of these jobs lasted, nor did his marriage. There was little alternative but to go where there was a demand for labour, which in Goate's case was the shipyards of the North-East.

For twenty-two years, William worked for Palmer's, the Jarrow shipbuilder. He also served for many years with the Jarrow Company of Volunteers in the same rank as he held in the cavalry. Age and illness ended his working life and, like many Victorian heroes from the ranks, he fell into deep poverty.

In May 1900, he left Tyneside and took up residence at 22 Leopold Street, Southsea, to be close to his son and young family. People who knew him at this time remarked on his strong resemblance to the then current hero, Lord Roberts. Within a year, William contracted gastric cancer and died at his home on 26 October 1901.

Goate was buried in a pauper's grave at the Highland Road Cemetery in Southsea (Plot E, Row 5, Common Grave 20).[10] By a tragic twist of fate, Goate's son, William, died in the Royal Naval Hospital, Haslar, and was buried on 29 November 1904 in the same grave as his father. Goate's Victoria Cross was auctioned by Glendining's in 1902 for £85. In 1950, the same firm resold the cross for £90. Eventually, William Goate's medals, the VC and three-bar Indian Mutiny medal, were sold at Sotheby's for £26,000 and are now on display in the 9/12th Royal Lancers Museum in Derby.

GUNN, George Ward
Rank/Service: 2nd Lieutenant, 3rd Regiment, Royal Horse Artillery
Other Decorations: MC
VC Location: Royal Artillery Museum, Woolwich
Date of Gazette: 21 April 1942
Place/Date of Birth: Muggleswick, Co. Durham, 26 July 1912
Place/Date of Death: Sidi Rezegh, Western Desert, 21 November 1941
Grave: Knightsbridge War Cemetery, Acroma, Libya
Town/County Connections: Neston, Wirral, Cheshire

Account of Deed: On 21 November 1941 at Sidi Rezegh, Libya, an attack by sixty German tanks was countered by four anti-tank guns under the command of 2nd Lieutenant Gunn. During the engagement, this officer drove from gun to gun in an unarmoured vehicle, encouraging his men, and when three of his guns were destroyed and the crew of the fourth, except the sergeant, were all dead or disabled, he took charge of this remaining weapon, the porte of which was alight. There was danger of the flames exploding the ammunition with which the porte was loaded, but he managed to fire fifty rounds and set two enemy tanks on fire before he himself was killed.

Biographical Detail: Ward Gunn's grandparents were Scottish and emigrated to Australia where Ward Gunn's father, named George, was born in Melbourne and educated at Melbourne Grammar School. However, he returned to Scotland to study medicine at Edinburgh and qualified in 1905. After various posts there and in Liverpool, he obtained the degree of Doctor of Medicine three years later and also became a Fellow of the Royal College of Surgeons of Edinburgh. He then worked for a period in Cairo where he met his future wife, who came from a distinguished Durham family. They returned England and he set up as a general practitioner in Neston.

George Ward Gunn was born at his grandparents' house Calf Hall, Muggleswick, in Co. Durham, possibly because the family home in Neston was still being built. He was educated at Parkgate at Mostyn House School, of which his father, amongst other institutions, was the medical officer.

Later, he and his three brothers boarded at Sedbergh School, Cumbria. They were collectively known as the 'Gunn Battery'. He did well at cricket and cross-country running. His Cadet Force record is not available but his brothers were all good at shooting.

After leaving school, he trained as an accountant in London and Liverpool, passing his final examinations in 1938. He became a chartered accountant and company secretary with Messrs. Sissons & Co. Ltd, chartered accountants of New Board Street, London.

He volunteered on the first day of the war, joining the Royal Artillery and was commissioned in 1940. He was part of the 7th Armoured Division (The Desert Rats) and was involved in the successful campaign from Egypt in 1940 and early 1941, winning a MC at the Battle of Bardia.

He was commemorated in Neston by the endowment of a bed in the local cottage hospital following an oversubscribed public appeal. A plaque to him over the bed was later transferred to St Mary's and St Helen's church when the hospital closed. In Neston itself, Gunn Grove is named after him and his picture hangs in the Royal British Legion building. Gunn is buried in the Knightsbridge Cemetery outside Tobruk. His medals are kept in the Royal Artillery Museum.

George Ward Gunn never married. Soldiering and medicine appear to have run in the family: a younger brother was a medical officer with the SAS in the early years of the Second World War and died in a car accident in 1944. Another brother was a doctor with the Chindits in Burma and went on to become an eminent orthopaedic surgeon after the war.

GUY, Basil John Douglas
Rank/Service: Midshipman (later Commander), Royal Navy
Other Decorations: DSO
VC Location: Lord Ashcroft VC Collection
Date of Gazette: 1 January 1901
Place/Date of Birth: Bishop Auckland, Co. Durham, 9 May 1882
Place/Date of Death: London, 29 December 1956
Grave: St Michael & All Saints, Pirbright, Surrey;
Memorials: Family Memorial Christ Church, Harrogate
Town/County Connections: Bishop Auckland, Co. Durham; Pirbright, Surrey; Harrogate, Yorkshire

Significant Remarks: Served in both World Wars.

Account of Deed: On 13 July 1900 during the attack on Tientsin, China, a very heavy crossfire was brought to bear on the Naval Brigade and there were several casualties. Among those who fell was an able seaman, shot about 50 yards short of cover. Midshipman Guy stopped with him and tried, unsuccessfully, to lift him up, so after bandaging his wound he ran to get help; during this time, the enemy were concentrating their fire on the two men. Shortly after Guy got under cover the stretchers arrived, and he again ran out and helped to bring in the wounded man, who was unfortunately shot again and died before he could be got to safety.

Biographical Detail: The son of the vicar of Christchurch, Harrogate, he was born at Bishop Auckland, Co. Durham. He was educated at Aysgarth School in Yorkshire, Llandaff Cathedral School in South Wales, and on board HMS *Britannia*, passing out to the *Barfleur* on 15 July 1898. He served in the Far East for many years, and took part in the Boxer Rebellion.

King Edward VII presented Guy with his VC on 8 March 1902 at Keyham Barracks, Devonport. He also received the China Medal and, on 15 July 1903, was promoted to Lieutenant.

He served in both World Wars, winning the DSO in the First World War for his command of a decoy ship HMS *Wonganella*. He was promoted to Commander in 1918. He died in London.

HEAVISIDE, Michael Wilson
Rank/Service: Private, 15th Battalion, Durham Light Infantry
VC Location: Durham Light Infantry Museum, Durham
Date of Gazette: 8 June 1917
Place/Date of Birth: Durham, 20 October 1880
Place/Date of Death: Durham, 26 April 1939
Grave: St Thomas's churchyard, Craghead (erected 1999)
Town/County Connections: Durham

Account of Deed: On 6 May 1917 near Fontaine-les-Croiselles, France, a wounded man was seen at about 2pm, in a shell hole some 40 yards from the enemy line. It was impossible to rescue him during daylight, but Private Heaviside volunteered to take water and food to him. This he succeeded in doing, in spite of heavy gunfire, and found that the man was nearly demented with thirst and had been lying in the shell hole for four days and three nights. The arrival of the water undoubtedly saved his life. Private Heaviside succeeded the same evening, with the help of two companions, in rescuing the man.

Biographical Detail: Michael Wilson Heaviside was born on 28 October 1880 at Station Lane, Gilesgate, in Durham City. His father, John Wilson Heaviside was, at that time, a grocer. When Michael was still a boy, the family moved to Kimblesworth, where his father worked as head keeper and Michael went to the local council school. Later, the family moved to Sacriston, when his father transferred to the local pit. Following the death of his mother, Annie, Michael enlisted as 11796 Private Heaviside in the Royal Army Medical Corps (RAMC). He served as a stretcher bearer in South Africa during the Boer War and was awarded the Queen's and King's South African Medals, before he was invalided home suffering from enteric fever.

After he left the Regular Army, Michael transferred to the Army Reserve and began work underground at Burnhope Colliery. He met his future wife, Elizabeth, whilst living in Burnhope and they married at Lanchester.

About 1913, he took work as a hewer at Oswald pit and the family moved to Craghead, near Stanley.

On 7 September 1914, with the First World War just a month old, 4/9720 Private Michael Heaviside re-enlisted, just one amongst the thousands of miners from Co. Durham who answered Kitchener's call. After training, he crossed to France in June 1915 and there settled into the deadly routine of trench warfare on the Western Front. He was 36 years old when at the Battle of Arras he won his Victoria Cross.

The battle began on Easter Monday, 9 April 1917, when the British Army attacked the complex system of trenches and barbed wire called the Hindenburg Line. That afternoon, as part of the 64th Brigade of the 21st Division, the 15th (Service) Battalion DLI advanced across a thousand yards of open ground, through two belts of wire and into the German front-line trench. The second line, however, was strongly defended with uncut barbed wire and machine guns. The battalion failed to advance any further, but was able to prevent the Germans from retaking their old front-line trench. In just two days, 15th DLI suffered over two hundred men killed or wounded before the battalion was taken out of the line to rest.

The 15th DLI returned to the battle on 3 May, when the battalion was ordered to attack down the Hindenburg Line near Fontaine-les-Croiselles. Here, both British and German troops held the same trench lines and only barricades kept the two forces apart. At 4am, after a fierce bombardment of the German barricades, bombers from the 15th DLI stormed the German positions. Once again, however, thick belts of barbed wire and machine guns held up the attackers. A British tank arrived about 5am and began to fire down the German held trench, but it was soon crippled by mortar fire. For the rest of the morning, fierce fighting raged around the barricades. In this unsuccessful action, the battalion suffered over one hundred casualties, including thirty men missing in the confusion. That afternoon, the 15th DLI was relieved and moved back to rest.

On the evening of 5 May 1917, the battalion returned to their barricades on the Hindenburg Line, near Fontaine-les-Croiselles. Only one hundred yards separated the British and German positions but the terrible fighting of the preceding days had died down. Snipers and machine-gunners were, however, still active and any movement attracted deadly fire. Then about 2pm the next afternoon, 6 May 1917, a sentry noticed movement in a shell hole about 40 yards from the German barricade. A wounded British soldier was desperately waving an empty water bottle. Any attempt to help this soldier in daylight would result in almost certain death for the rescuers. Michael Heaviside, however, said that he was going to try. Grabbing water and a first aid bag, this 36–year-old stretcher bearer scrambled over the barricade and out into no-man's-land. Immediately, he came under heavy rifle and machine-gun fire from the German positions and was forced to throw himself to the ground. He then began to crawl 60 yards across the broken ground from shell hole to shell hole to where the wounded soldier was sheltering. One eye witness later wrote: 'We could see bullets striking the ground right around the spot over which Heaviside was crawling. Every minute we expected to be his last but the brave chap went on.' As he crawled closer to the German lines, the firing increased. 'The enemy seemed to be more determined to hit him, for the bullets were spluttering about more viciously than ever.'

When Private Heaviside reached the soldier, he found the man nearly demented with thirst for he had been lying badly wounded in the shell hole for four days and three nights, without any food or water. Michael Heaviside gave the soldier water, dressed his wounds and then promised that he would return with help. That night, Michael Heaviside led two other stretcher bearers out across no-man's-land to the wounded soldier and carried him back to safety. Without doubt, he had saved this man's life.

The London Gazette announced the award of the Victoria Cross to Private Michael Heaviside on 8 June 1917 for his 'most conspicuous bravery and devotion to duty'. He was the third soldier of the Durham Light Infantry to gain this award during the First World War.

The next day, a local reporter went to see Elizabeth Heaviside and found her sitting on the doorstep of her home in Front Street, Craghead, nursing her youngest child and reading about her husband's bravery. The whole village was talking about 'Mick's success'.

Private M W Heaviside VC returned home to a hero's welcome. Shield Row railway station was crowded with excited people as the 6.13pm train from Newcastle steamed in on time and a great cheer went up as a soldier wearing khaki uniform and cap and carrying a rifle and steel helmet stepped down on to the platform to be met by his father, three of his young children and local dignitaries.

Then outside to waiting cars and a procession led by South Moor Colliery Band, 'D' Company of the 1st Battalion Durham County Volunteers from Stanley and Church Lads Brigade Cadets from Beamish. As the band struck up 'See the Conquering Hero Comes', the cars moved off through crowded streets hung with flags and bunting towards Stanley Town Hall for speeches and yet more cheering. Then on to South Moor, passing 'Welcome Home' banners, until finally, about 7.45pm, the procession stopped at Craghead football ground. There, after more speeches, the band played 'For He's a Jolly Good Fellow' and the children of Craghead and Bloemfontein Council Schools sang 'Rule Britannia'. Craghead had never seen anything like it. It was Thursday 12 July 1917 and Private Michael Heaviside was home not simply on leave but to be presented with the Victoria Cross for saving a man's life.

Following the memorable 'Welcome Home' parade, Michael Heaviside was presented, during another enthusiastic public meeting at Craghead football field, with a gold watch and chain and War Bonds. After the presentation, he told the crowd that he had only done his duty and that he was proud to have brought honour to Durham and to Craghead, in particular. A few days later, on 21 July 1917, Private Michael Heaviside travelled by train to London and, in the forecourt of Buckingham Palace, was presented with his Victoria Cross by King George V.

After the war, Michael Heaviside VC returned to work as a miner at Craghead. On 26 June 1920 he was among the guests who attended King George V's afternoon garden party held at Buckingham Palace for recipients of the Victoria Cross.

On 26 April 1939, he died at his home at Bloemfontein Terrace, aged just 58 years, his health damaged by his years underground and his time on the Western Front.

Hundreds of mourners, many wearing their Great War medals, followed Michael Heaviside's coffin to St Thomas's church, Craghead, as the local colliery band played the 'Dead March in Saul'. At the graveside, a firing party from the 8th Battalion DLI fired three volleys of shots, followed by the 'Last Post' played by the battalion's buglers, then the mourners filed past, each dropping Flanders poppies into the open grave.

Finally, on 12 July 1957, forty years after his 'Welcome Home' parade through the streets of Stanley and Craghead, Michael Heaviside's Victoria Cross and other medals were presented by his family to the Durham Light Infantry's Regimental Museum. This presentation took place during a parade at Brancepeth Castle, when, watched by his mother and over thirty relatives of Michael Heaviside VC, Company Sergeant Major Norman Heaviside proudly handed over his father's medals.

KENNY, Thomas

Rank / Service: Private (later Lance-Sgt), 13th En, Durham Light Infantry
VC Location: Private (not on public display)
Date of Gazette: 7 December 1915
Place / Date of Birth: South Wingate. Co. Durham, 4 April 1882
Place / Date of Death: Durham, 29 November 1958
Grave: Wheatley Hill Cemetery (erected 1994)
Town / County Connections: South Wingate, Co. Durham

Account of Deed: On 4 November 1915 near La Houssoie. France, in thick mist, an officer in charge of a patrol was shot through both thighs. Private Kenny, although repeatedly fired on by the enemy, crawled about for more than an hour with his wounded officer on his back, trying to find his way through the fog to British trenches. He refused to leave the officer, although told several times to do so, and at last, utterly exhausted, left him in a comparatively safe ditch and went for help. He found a rescue party and guided them to the wounded officer who was then brought to safety.

Biographical Detail: Thomas Kenny was born at South Wingate, Co. Durham on 4 April 1882. After he left St Mary's Roman Catholic School at Wingate, he worked as a quarryman and, later, as a miner. By 1914 he was married to Isabel (née Applegarth) and they had six children, all living in a small terrace house in Walker's Building in South Wingate.

On 16 September 1914, the new recruits for the 13th (Service) Battalion DLI were sent south by train from Newcastle upon Tyne to Bullswater Camp, near Pirbright in Surrey to become part of the 68th Brigade of the 23rd Division. There began the difficult task of turning enthusiastic civilians into trained soldiers. This job was made more difficult by the lack of instructors, experienced officers and non-commissioned officers. Added to this was the shortage of uniforms, rifles and equipment, and the dreadful state of the camp at Bullswater. The battalion lived in tents until the end of November and suffered badly from the rain, mud and cold. Finally at the end of July 1915, all ranks were given seven days' leave. Training was over. Active service on the Western Front was about to begin.

Private Thomas Kenny, 17424, 'B' Company, 13th (Service) Battalion DLI landed at Boulogne with his battalion on 26 August 1915, nearly a year after he had volunteered. They then marched about 50 miles east toward the Belgian border where on 7 October the 13th DLI relieved the 12th (Service) Battalion DLI in the line at Bois Grenier, near Armentieres. This part of the Western Front was described in 1915 as 'quiet', though the battalion still suffered daily casualties from shelling, rifle grenades and snipers.

A vivid description of these first few weeks of the battalion's life in the trenches survives in the letters Lieutenant Philip Anthony Brown wrote home to his mother. He was born in 1886 in Kent and studied history at Oxford, before moving to Newcastle upon Tyne in 1911 as a tutor with the Workers' Educational Association, The following year he became a lecturer at Durham University. When the Great War began, he enlisted as a private but was soon persuaded to accept a commission in the 13th Battalion DLI. On 8 October 1915, he wrote:

> About 12.30am, a man came and said he could hear moaning over the parapet. I was afraid that this meant that some of my men, who had just started on a listening patrol, had been hit … I went down with my observer, a very nice Irishman from County Durham, who goes with me everywhere, and crept along … a very shallow trench. We soon came on one man down in the bottom of the ditch. It was difficult to move him, but finally my observer got him on his back. Poor fellow had a bad wound in the side.

This was the first night of the battalion's first tour of duty in the trenches. The observer was Private Thomas Kenny. The routine of front-line duty followed by relief continued for the rest of October, with working parties – digging and wiring – sent out every night, except when it was so wet that all work was cancelled. About 8.30pm on 2 November, in pouring rain, the 13th Battalion relieved the 12th DLI, once again, in the front-line trenches numbered 1.26.3–5, opposite La Houssoie, near Armentieres. The rain continued all the next day, filling the trenches and caving in the parapets and dugouts, but at least the rain kept the Germans quiet.

Philip Brown wrote again to his mother:

We have gone back to the trenches – and to such trenches. I don't think any words can adequately describe them. It has been raining … There is not a patch of dry ground anywhere. Boards soaked in mud, sandbags bursting with mud, ponds and even wells of mud … yellow mud, greasy ponds, dirty clothes and heaps of mangled sandbags. A great deal of the trench work is collapsing in the wet, as was to be expected, and it keeps us busy reconstructing it. We had a certain amount of shellfire, but very little rifle fire yet. A mild enemy in front of us, I think. Now I must stop, as I am on duty and should go the rounds.

This was his last letter home.

At 9.15pm on 4 November 1915, Lieutenant Brown, as the officer of the watch, went out to visit a party working on the barbed wire in front of Trench 1.26.4. He was accompanied, as always, by his observer, Private Thomas Kenny. The rain had stopped, but with no wind, a thick fog covered no-man's-land. In the dark and fog, Lieutenant Brown lost his bearings and missed the working party. The two soldiers went on until they realised that the ground was unfamiliar. They were lost somewhere in no-man's-land. They then sat down to listen for any sounds that might direct them back to their own lines and safety. Hearing nothing, they decided to try to retrace their steps through the mud. It was then about 9.45pm. At the moment they rose, a single rifle shot rang out and Lieutenant Brown fell, shot through both thighs.

Thomas Kenny at once went to his aid and hoisted Lieutenant Brown onto his back. Immediately, heavy rifle fire opened up from the German lines, forcing Private Kenny to crawl through the mud, but still he kept his badly wounded officer on his back. When the bursts of fire were too severe, he lay still, only starting again when the firing slackened. This ordeal lasted for nearly an hour, before Private Kenny, cold, wet and utterly exhausted, at last stumbled upon a ditch he recognised. He made Lieutenant Brown as comfortable as he could and started off to find his battalion's front line.

Kenny arrived at a battalion listening post in Trench 1.26.4 at just after 11pm, and there found Captain White. After he heard Kenny's story, Captain White asked for volunteers to go with him out into no-man's-land. Two stretcher bearers, plus Privates Thomas Kerr and Michael Prough volunteered. Private Kenny, despite his exhaustion, his torn uniform and his bleeding hands and legs, then led them to where he had left his wounded officer. As the rescue party started back with Lieutenant Brown for their own lines, German soldiers opened fire with rifles and machine-guns and then grenades were thrown from a position only 30 yards away. Captain White immediately ordered the party to go on, whilst he stayed behind to cover their retreat. All reached safety without suffering any further casualty.

Once back in the battalion's trenches, Philip Brown, despite his terrible wounds and weak from loss of blood, recovered consciousness for a short time and was heard to say – 'Well, Kenny, you're a hero, now.' He died whilst he was being carried back to the dressing station.

The *London Gazette* announced the award of the Victoria Cross to Private Thomas Kenny, on 7 December 1915, stating that his 'pluck, endurance and devotion to duty were beyond praise'. He was the first soldier of the Durham Light Infantry to gain this award during the First World War. On 4 March 1916, Lance Sergeant Thomas Kenny was presented with this Victoria Cross by King George V at Buckingham Palace. Mrs Brown, the mother of Philip Brown, was there to meet the man who had tried so hard and for so long to save her son's life.

Briefly Sergeant Kenny returned to Wingate on leave to his wife and family – which by now had increased to seven children. The *Northern Echo* made much of his exploits, and before a full house at the Palace Theatre, the manager of Wingate Colliery presented Thomas and his wife with £50 in War Bonds, which had been raised by local people, and then he visited his old school as guest of honour. At that event he was presented with a marble clock, a pipe and some tobacco, after which the pupils read out a poem.

> Welcome, welcome once again
> Hero brave and bold
> To the school where you were taught
> In the days of old.
>
> We the present pupils of Wingate Catholic School
> Were pleased to hear
> When death was near
> You were so brave and cool.

Thomas Kenny returned to his battalion on the Western Front for Christmas. He was wounded in October 1916 and, by 1918, had risen to the rank of Company Sergeant Major.

With the end of the First World War came demobilisation, Thomas Kenny returned to his wife and children and his old life as a miner.

On 26 June 1920 Thomas Kenny was among the guests who attended King George V's afternoon garden party held at Buckingham Palace for recipients of the Victoria Cross.

Kenny remained at Wingate Colliery until 1927 and then moved a few miles to 13 Darlington Street, Wheatley Hill, and took a job in the local colliery as a stone man drifter. He continued to work underground until 1944, when, aged 62 years, after a shoulder injury, he finally moved to a surface job. At this time, Thomas and his family attended Thornley Roman Catholic Church.

Thomas Kenny VC died in Durham on 29 November 1948, aged 66, and was buried, on 2 December, at Wheatley Hill Cemetery, Co. Durham. Following an appeal by members of the 'Faithful' Inkerman Club, his unmarked grave was finally given a headstone in August 1994. The stone was unveiled by Captain Richard Annand VC, during a simple ceremony.

KIBBY, William Henry

Rank/Service: Sergeant, 2/48th Bn, AIF (SA), Australian Military Forces
VC Location: Australian War Memorial, Anzac Parade, Canberra
Date of Gazette: 28 January 1943
Place/Date of Birth: Winlaton, Co. Durham, 15 April 1903
Place/Date of Death: Miteiriya Ridge, Libya, 31 October 1942
Grave: El Alamein War Cemetery, Egypt, Row XVI, Plot C, Grave 26
Memorials: Australian War Memorial, Canberra: Jubilee 150 Walkway
    plaque commemorating Second World War heroes

Significant Remarks: Although born in Co. Durham he always considered
himself Australian.

Account of Deed: At the Battle of El Alamein, during the period of 23–31
October 1942, Kibby distinguished himself through his skill in leading
a platoon, after his commander had been killed, during the initial attack
at Miteiriya Ridge. On 23 October, he charged a machine-gun position,
firing at it with his Thompson sub-machine-gun; Kibby killed three
enemy soldiers, captured twelve others and took the position. His company
commander intended to recommend him for the Distinguished Conduct
Medal after this action, but was killed. During the following days, Kibby
moved among his men directing fire and cheering them on. He mended
his platoon's telephone line several times under intense fire. On 30–31
October, the platoon came under intense machine-gun and mortar fire.
Most of them were killed or wounded. In order to achieve his company's
objective, Kibby moved forward alone, to within a few metres of the enemy,
throwing grenades to destroy them. Just as his success in this endeavour
appeared certain, he was killed.

Biographical Detail: 'Bill' Kibby was born at Winlaton, Co. Durham.
He arrived in Adelaide, Australia, from Britain with his parents in 1914.
Here Bill attended Mitcham Public School. At this period he was also a
Boy Scout with the 2nd Glenelg Sea Scouts. After leaving school he was
employed at a plasterworks in Edwardstown, where he designed and fixed

plaster decorations. In 1926, he married Mabel Sarah Bidmead Morgan; they lived at Helmsdale and had two daughters.

Although he was considered diminutive, standing only 5′ 6″, Kibby was a strong man and loved outdoor activities. In 1936, he joined the Militia, and was assigned to the 48 Field Battery, Royal Australian Artillery.

In 1940 he embarked with the 2/48th Battalion from Adelaide, bound for the Middle East. Following an accident which resulted in a leg injury, he rejoined his battalion before the Battle of El Alamein.

When the body of Sergeant Kibby was recovered several days after his death, riddled with bullets, he was only yards from the machine-gun and the enemy gun crew were all dead. Close by was the body of his Company Commander, Captain Peter Roberts. In his pocket was a note recommending Kibby for the VC.

The Victoria Cross medal was presented to his widow by Brigadier General the Right Honourable Alexander Gore Arkwright Hore-Ruthven, 1st Baron Gowrie VC, GCMG, CB, DSO, Governor General of Australia, on 27 November 1943.

It is now held by the Australian War Memorial, Anzac Parade, Canberra, Australian Capital Territory, Australia.

William Kibby was buried in the field but his body was later exhumed and reburied in El Alamein War Cemetery, Egypt, on 15 January 1944. Plot No. XVI. Row A. Grave 18. An Army Club at Woodside Camp, South Australia, was named after him.

McKEAN, George Burden
Rank/Service: Lieut. (later Captain), 14111 En, Quebec Regiment, CEF
Other Decorations: MC, MM
VC Location: Canadian War Museum, Ottawa
Date of Gazette: 28 June 1918
Place/Date of Birth: Willington, Bishop Auckland, Co. Durham, 4 July 1888
Place/Date of Death: Brighton, East Sussex, 28 November 1926
Grave: Brighton Extra-Mural Cemetery, Sussex
Memorials: Canadian War Museum; on 6 September 2003, the Church
   Square of Cagnicourt, France, was renamed 'La Place George Burdon
   McKean' in his honour.
Town/County Connections: Willington, Bishop Auckland, Co. Durham;
   Cuffley, Herts; Brighton, Sussex

Account of Deed: On 27/28 April 1918 at the Gavrelle Sector, France, when
Lieutenant McKean's party was held up at a block in the communication
trench by intense fire, he ran into the open, leaping over the block head first
on top of one of the enemy. Whilst he was lying there, another with a fixed
bayonet attacked him; he shot both of these men, captured the position,
then sent back for more bombs. Until they arrived, he engaged the enemy
single-handed. He then rushed a second block, killing two of the enemy,
capturing four others, and then proceeded to drive the remainder into a
dugout, which he then destroyed.

Biographical Detail: McKean was born in Willington, Co. Durham, the
son of James McKean and Jane Ann (née Henderson).[11] Little is known
of his parents or early life but it is known that he was orphaned young. It
is also known that he was a member of a Boy Scout troop while living in
Durham. George emigrated to Canada in 1902 at the age of 14 to join his
elder brother J W McKean. The delay in joining his sibling may have been
due to the fact that he had had a 'virulent' form of TB that the sanatorium
considered incurable and which meant spending two years on his back
during treatment. During the time of his illness, he lived with his sister in
Bishop Auckland.

On arriving in Canada McKean first worked on his brother's cattle ranch and farm near Lethbridge, Alberta. After some years of farming, he moved to the Connaught area of Calgary where in 1912 he enrolled at Robertson College, the Presbyterian theological college in Edmonton. During summers he served as a student missionary at Hardieville and Athabasca Landing, and was an assistant pastor at Robertson Presbyterian Church where in 1913 he organised the first Boy Scout troop at the church.

In 1915 George married Isabel Hall, just at the time of his enlistment: she worked as a private secretary in the office of Major J M Carson, the military registrar in Calgary.

George had tried to join up but been rejected three times before he was accepted as a private in the 51st Infantry Battalion not long after his marriage. Interestingly, he gave his occupation on enlisting as 'schoolteacher'. Possibly his initial rejections were due to his height and size as he only stood 5' 6" inches and weighed 120 pounds. As part of the Canadian Expeditionary Force he arrived in England as a sergeant in 1916 and, after transferring to the 14th Infantry Battalion (the Royal Montreal regiment), he was sent to France as a private in June 1916. When he won the Military Medal (MM) at Bully-Grenay, near Lens, he had had advanced to the rank of corporal, and was subsequently recommended for a commission, which he obtained in April 1917.

For a period Captain McKean fought as a military scout with the Canadians in occupied France and his Boy Scout experience both back in Co. Durham and in Edmonton stood him in good stead – the motto was the same: be prepared.

Severely wounded, McKean was invalided back to England and was unable to rejoin his regiment before the end of the war. During his convalescence, and while he was still in a bad way, Frederick Horsman Varley, one of Canada's war artists, painted his portrait. Of this haunting work, the artist's son Peter wrote, 'In his characterisation of McKean, Varley caught the numbed horror of his shattered soul: rigid, staring, one eye showing a wild defiance, almost rage; the other guarded, cynical, hiding a storm of hatred.'

While recovering McKean wrote *Scouting Thrills*, based on his wartime exploits and scouting skills; this was published in 1919. 'We were forever scraping up a lively acquaintance with the Hun,' he wrote. 'We found, as I hope these stories prove, that he was woefully lacking in a spirit of adventure.' Later he drew on his time in Canada for a children's book *Making Good: A Story of North-West Canada* (London, 1920). This was a tale of two English lads' adventures ranching in Alberta.

On 26 June 1920 McKean was among the guests who attended King George V's afternoon garden party held at Buckingham Palace for recipients of the Victoria Cross.

On his release from hospital in February 1919 Captain McKean was put in charge of the Bureau of Information at the Khaki University of Canada in London, an educational scheme initiated by the Canadian YMCA to prepare soldiers for civilian life. Soon after, in July, McKean retired from the forces himself. He married an English girl Constance (unknown) and they produced a daughter, settling near Brighton. In 1926 the sawmill he was operating at Cuffley, north of London, flew apart. After surviving four years of war he was killed in this dreadful accident when a piece of the circular saw blade became embedded in his skull.

In 1979 George McKean's widow Constance sold his medals and a world record price was achieved when the set of three realised £17,000, twice the previous best, at Sotheby's. Sadly, the decision to sell his awards caused a serious family row. Today his medals and portrait are held by the Canadian War Museum in Ottawa.

The computer suite in the Willington Partnership offices is now named in his memory.

McNALLY, William
Rank/Service: Sergeant, 8th (S) Bn, Yorkshire Regiment (Alexandra, Princess of Wales's Own)
Other Decorations: MM & Bar
VC Location: Green Howard's Regimental Museum, Richmond
Date of Gazette: 14 December 1918
Place/Date of Birth: Murton, nr. Seaham, Co. Durham, 16 December 1894
Place/Date of Death: Murton, nr. Seaham, Co. Durham, 5 January 1976
Grave: Tyne & Wear Crematorium, Sunderland
Memorials: Stone memorial in small public park at Murton.
Town/County Connections: Murton, Co. Durham

Account of Deed: For most conspicuous bravery and skilful leading during the operations on the 27 October 1918, across the river Piave, in north-east Italy, when his company was most seriously hindered in its advance by heavy machine-gun fire from the vicinity of some buildings on a flank. Utterly regardless of personal safety, he rushed the machine-gun post single-handed, killing the team and capturing the gun. Later at Vassola, on 29 October, when his company, having crossed the Monticano River, came under heavy rifle fire and machine-gun fire, Sergeant McNally directed the fire of his platoon against the danger point, while he himself crept to the rear of the enemy's position. Realising that a frontal attack would mean heavy losses, he rushed the position unaided, killing or putting to flight the garrison and capturing a machine-gun. On the same day, when holding a newly captured ditch, he was strongly counter-attacked from both flanks. By his coolness and skill in controlling the fire of his party he frustrated the attack, inflicting heavy casualties on the enemy. Throughout the whole of the operations, his innumerable acts of gallantry set a high example to his men, and his leading was beyond all praise.

Biographical Detail: William McNally was born at 12 Bude Square, Murton, near Seaham, Co. Durham on 16 December 1894. At the age of 4, he went to Murton Colliery School but left, aged 14, to follow his father down the pits as a pit pony boy. He worked six shifts a week until he was 20 years old. On 3 September 1914, he enlisted in Sunderland into the Green Howards. After training he was posted to the 8th (Service) Battalion, the Yorkshire Regiment, at Halton Park Camp in Buckinghamshire. They trained for a year before travelling to France in August 1915 as part of 69 Brigade, 23rd Division.

As a private, he was awarded his first Military Medal on 10 July 1916 for bravery at Contalmaison during the Battle of the Somme, which was gazetted on 23 August 1916. He went to the assistance of an officer who was wounded in the thigh and dragged him back to safety.

On 3 November 1917, he won a bar to his Military Medal for bravery near Passchendale. On three separate occasions, he rescued men who had been wounded or buried by enemy shellfire in the trenches. It was not gazetted until 23 February 1918. In mid-November 1917, the 8th Yorkshires were sent from the Western Front to Northern Italy. It was here between 27 and 29 October 1918 that 13820 Sergeant William McNally MM performed three separate acts of gallantry which won him the Victoria Cross. The citation appeared in the *London Gazette* on 14 December 1918.

In February 1919, Billy McNally left the Army at Ripon still suffering from his third wound, a bullet in the leg, but it did not prevent him from returning home to work down the coal mine at Murton Colliery. He was a member of the Miner's Lodge Committee and in 1947 became a timber-yard foreman making pit props. He retired at the age of 65 in July 1958.

He got married just before receiving the VC from George V at Buckingham Palace on 17 July 1919. On 26 June 1920 William McNally was among the guests who attended King George V's afternoon garden party held at Buckingham Palace for recipients of the Victoria Cross, and similarly, on 26 June 1956, he attended the Hyde Park VC Reunion. He was also present at the second reunion dinner of the Victoria Cross Association and Associate members of the George Cross held on Thursday, 7 July 1960, at the Café Royal in London at which the loyal toast was proposed by the Chairman Brigadier Sir John Smyth, Bt. C, MC, MP and a toast to 'Our Guests' was made by the Association Vice-Chairman, the Revd Geoffrey Woolley VC, OBE, MC, MA.

In retirement, he lived for another sixteen years, taking an active part in the local community. He died at his place of birth on 5 January 1976. His ashes were scattered in Sunderland's Garden of Remembrance at the Tyne and Wear Crematorium.

In October 1978, his life was commemorated by a stone memorial in Murton Park near the village war memorial. The stone memorial was unveiled by his widow accompanied by their two sons and daughter. Mrs McNally presented her husband's Victoria Cross, Military Medal and bar, and six medals to the regiment in 1979.

The Cenotaph in Whitehall was completed shortly after the end of the 1914–18 War and was scheduled to be unveiled by King George V on Armistice Day 1920. However, in October of that year the Dean of Westminster suggested to Buckingham Palace that the body of an unidentified soldier be exhumed from the battlefields and reburied in Westminster Abbey. To ensure the warrior was unknown, the military authorities on the old Western Front were instructed to exhume six unidentified 'British' soldiers. On 9 November 1920, six working parties commanded by subalterns, went to the six main battlefields – Aisne, Arras, Cambrai, Marne, Somme and Ypres – each to exhume the remains of one soldier buried in a grave marked 'Unknown'.

The six bodies were put in coffins and taken to a hut near Ypres where they were received by a clergyman. A blindfolded officer went inside the hut and at random touched the coffin of the soldier who was to be laid among kings in Westminster Abbey. The body was brought across the English Channel from Boulogne to Dover on HMS *Verdun*. Following a brief service the Unknown Warrior was lowered into his grave near the Great West Door on 11 November 1920, the grave refilled with earth brought from the battlefields.

The order of the service in Westminster Abbey was published in *The Times* newspaper on Tuesday, 9 November 1920, and concluded: 'The Unknown Warrior will be carried to his last resting place in Westminster Abbey between two lines of men who won the Victoria Cross or who had otherwise distinguished themselves by special valour during World War I. These will include representatives of the Royal Navy, the Army, and the Royal Air Force.' The bodyguard of those heroes included Sergeant William McNally VC, MM, of the Yorkshire regiment.

MALING, George Allen
Rank/Service: T/Lieutenant (later Captain), Royal Army Medical Corps,
attd 12th Bn, The Rifle Brigade (Prince Consort's Own)
VC Location: Army Medical Services Museum, Mytchett
Date of Gazette: 18 November 1915
Place/Date of Birth: Sunderland, Co. Durham, 6 October 1888
Place/Date of Death: Lee, London, 9 July 1929
Grave: Chistlehurst Cemetery, Kent
Town/County Connections: Sunderland, Co. Durham; London

Account of Deed: On 25 September 1915, near Fauquissart, France,
Lieutenant Maling worked for over twenty-four hours with untiring
energy, collecting and treating in the open, under heavy shellfire, more
than 300 men. During the morning of the 25th the bursting of a large
high-explosive shell that wounded his only assistant and killed several of
his patients temporarily stunned him. A second shell covered him and his
instruments with debris, but he continued his gallant work single-handed
against almost overwhelming adversity.

Biographical Detail: Born in 1888 George Allan Maling was part of the noted
Maling Pottery family. He was born in Bishopwearmouth, Co. Durham,
the son of Edwin Allan Maling (1838–1920), a general practitioner, and his
wife, Maria Jane, née Hartley (1847–1932). He was also a maternal cousin
of Sir Henry Havelock. At the time he enlisted in the Army, George Maling
was a practising doctor himself, and no doubt this influenced his choice
to enlist in the RAMC. Today, Maling's Victoria Cross is displayed at the
Army Medical Services Museum (Aldershot). His obituary was printed in
The Times on 29 July 1929:

> WE regret to record the death of Dr. George A. Malling, on July 9th,
> at his residence in Lee, S.E. London. George Allan Malling was the
> youngest son of Dr. E. A. Maling, J.P., of Blackwell Hall, Darlington.
> He was, born at Sunderland, in October, 1888, and after leaving
> Uppingham School studied medicine at the University of Oxford

and St. Thomas's Hospital. He graduated MB, B.Ch.Oxon in 1914, and in the following year took the diplomas M.R.C.S., L.R.C.P. He obtained a temporary commission in the R.A.M.C. in January, 1915, and five months later crossed to France, being attached to the 12th Battalion of the Rifle Brigade. It was announced in the *London Gazette* of November 15th, 1915, that the Victoria Cross had been conferred on him ...

Dr. Maling was also mentioned in despatches and was promoted to captain. He subsequently served for a short time at the Military Hospital, Grantham, and then returned to France for two years with the 34th Field Ambulance of the 11th Division.

After being demobilised at the end of the war he obtained the post of resident Medical Officer to the Victoria Hospital for Children, Chelsea. Sometime later he went into a medical partnership based at Micheldever Road, in Lee, South London where he practised until his death on 9 July 1929 aged 40. He also held an appointment as surgeon to out-patients at St. John's Hospital, Lewisham. On 5 May 1917 he married Daisy Mabel (née Wollmer) of Winnipeg, Canada, at Sutton in Surrey and they had one son.

MORRELL see YOUNG, Thomas

MURPHY, Michael
Rank/Service: Farrier (later Farrier Major), 2nd Engineer, Military Train
   (later Royal Army Service Corps)
VC Location: HQ RLC Officer's Mess, Camberley
Date of Gazette: 27 May 1859
Place/Date of Birth: Cahir, Tipperary, Ireland, 1831
Place/Date of Death: Darlington, Co. Durham, 4 April 1893
Grave: Darlington North Municipal Cemetery
Town/County Connections: Cahir, Tipperary; Darlington, Co. Durham

Account of Deed: On 15 April, 1858 during the pursuit of Koer Singh's rebel
army from Asimeghur, India, Farrier Murphy along with Private Samuel
Morley, also with the 2nd Battalion, went to the rescue of Lieutenant
Hamilton, Adjutant of the 3rd Sikh Cavalry, who had been wounded,
dismounted and was surrounded by the enemy. Morley and Farrier Murphy
cut down several of the enemy and the latter himself was severely wounded,
however this did not deter him and neither he nor Private Morley ever left
Lieutenant Hamilton's side until support arrived.

Interestingly, the Victoria Cross was awarded to Murphy, but not to
Private Morley. Private Morley felt somewhat aggrieved when he learned
that Farrier Murphy had been awarded the VC, when they had both been
involved in the rescue of the Lieutenant. Morley spoke to General Paget
CB of his grievance, during his inspection at Aldershot in 1860. The general
took up the complaint, read reports of the action, and on the evidence, the
powers that be decided that Morley should also receive the VC.

Biographical Detail: Michael Murphy was born c.1831[12] in Cahir, Tipperary,
to Michael Murphy, a local blacksmith, and his (unknown) wife. He had at
least one sibling, a younger sister named Mary. Little is known about his
early life until 1855, when he started his army career.

On 27 August 1855, Murphy enlisted in the 17th Lancers at Cork. The
17th Lancers, however, were still at the Crimean War, having lost most
of their complement in the Charge of the Light Brigade in the previous

year. As a result, Murphy started his training with the 16th Lancers at the Portobello Barracks, Dublin.

On 22 May 1856, Murphy attached to the 17th Lancers, who were now en route from the Crimea, via Ismid in Turkey, to help contain the early stages of the Indian Mutiny. It seems he intended to catch up with his regiment in India. Something must have affected this plan, since on 18 October 1856, he joined the 2nd Battalion Military Train (later the Royal Army Service Corps and nowadays the Royal Logistic Corps) instead. In March 1857, Murphy left the Curragh Camp and boarded the steamer *Calypso* at Dublin bound for Woolwich. On 28 April, he embarked for Hong Kong. On reaching Indonesia, the battalion was diverted to Calcutta on news of the Indian Mutiny. They arrived in Calcutta on 27 August, and after a series of moves were deployed to relieve Lucknow. The battalion was subsumed into the Azimghur Field Force on 29 March 1858.

After his injuries at Nathupur, Murphy was invalided to Calcutta and returned to the United Kingdom and the Invalid Depot, Great Yarmouth. On 14 May 1859, he resumed his duties at the Depot, at Aldershot and returned to the 2nd Battalion on 1 October 1859. Queen Victoria presented Michael Murphy with his Victoria Cross in the Quadrangle, Windsor Castle, on 4 January 1860. On 7 April 1860, he married at Aldershot and his new wife and two children joined him in establishment accommodation the same day. Murphy was soon promoted to Farrier-Sergeant, and moved to Woolwich. In January 1862, Murphy was attached to the 1st Battalion and served five months in Canada, returning on 14 June 1862 to Woolwich and then onto Aldershot. On 21 March 1865, Murphy transferred to the 6th Battalion and moved to the Royal Military Academy Sandhurst. On 6 September of the following year, Murphy rejoined the Military Train at the Curragh in Ireland. By 1868, he was back at Woolwich with his wife and two children. By the time the Military Train became the Army Service Corps in 1869, Murphy had achieved the rank of Farrier-Major and was stationed in Aldershot. On 1 July 1871, Murphy transferred from the Army Service Corps to the 7th Hussars.

On 26 January 1872, a civilian, James Green, was stopped by Farrier-Major Knott at Aldershot with a wagon containing sacks of oats and hay. Green stated that Murphy had given him permission to remove these goods. Murphy and Green were then arrested for the theft of these goods. At the trial at Winchester, Green was acquitted and released, but Murphy was convicted and sentenced to nine months' hard labour at the House of Correction for the county of Hampshire. On 5 March, an order was issued for the forfeit of Murphy's VC. Murphy was one of only eight men who forfeited their Victoria Crosses. Although Murphy had worn his Victoria Cross every day during his trial, the medal could not be found after the forfeiture order. His wife Mary and their child had disappeared from their Army establishment accommodation. After Murphy was released from prison on 30 November 1872, he returned to his regiment at Hounslow.

During 1873, Murphy's battalion moved to Wimbledon and then Maidstone. Murphy was in hospital and did not move with his battalion when it moved to Norwich in June 1874. His wife and children returned to Army establishment in December 1873. On 7 December 1874, Murphy was transferred to the 9th Lancers. In January 1875, the 9th Lancers were sent to Bombay, but Murphy reattached to the 5th Lancers returning from India. On 1 February 1875, after almost twenty years army service, Murphy was discharged at Colchester.

Immediately following his army discharge, Murphy took up residence in Bellingham, Northumberland. From Bellingham, he moved by early 1876 to become a blacksmith at Scotswood, Newcastle upon Tyne, then by mid-1878 to Murton, Co. Durham, where on 15 May 1878 their daughter Mary Ann was born, and, by 1881, back to Heworth, Northumberland.[13]

During the 1880s, Murphy's children appear to have left home. In 1889, while staying at Wilton Lodge, Darlington, Murphy's wife was admitted to Winterton Asylum, Sedgefield, where she later died on 3 March 1900. By 1891, Murphy had moved on his own to a cottage on the Blackwell Grange estate, outside Darlington[14] (owned by a benefactor, Sir Henry Havelock-Allan, another Victoria Cross recipient who also paid for a headstone for

Murphy). Murphy later relocated to Darlington to work as a labourer in an ironworks.

Murphy died of pneumonia at 22 Vulcan Street, Darlington on 4 April 1893.[15] He was buried in the North Road Municipal Cemetery, Darlington. A gravestone was erected by Sir Henry and comrades from the India campaign. Despite having at least two children still alive but not at home, his sole heir was stated to be Bridget Mary Anne Dobson,[16] a married niece who was caring for and residing with him at the end.

It is not known where the medal was kept between March 1872 and June 1898, or who held possession. However, five years after Murphy's death, in June 1898, his Victoria Cross medal eventually resurfaced when it was offered by an anonymous seller at auction. It was bought by Master Sergeant Masterman on behalf of the Royal Army Service Corps, at Aldershot. This medal was presented to the RASC, which has since been subsumed into the Royal Logistic Corps, based at the Princess Royal Barracks, Deepcut, Surrey. Murphy's actual medal is now owned by a regimental trust and can be viewed, but only by prior arrangement with the Royal Logistic Corps Museum.

Twenty-seven years after Murphy's death, in July 1920, the rules for the Victoria Cross award were changed to exclude forfeiture. The eight extant forfeits – including that of Murphy – were then relisted in the Victoria Cross register.

Michael Murphy married Mary Fox (born c.1841 Ireland, died 9 March 1900), daughter of a labourer named Bernard Fox, at the Farnham Register Office, near Aldershot, on 7 April 1860.[17] One or both of them may have had previous children, or may have been caring for family or army children, since the army records state that they went onto army establishment the very same day with two children or stepchildren, aged one year and five years. Subsequently, they had at least three children together: Edward John Murphy (b. 10 January 1864 Aldershot Camp – alive at 1881 Census – d. unknown); George Frederick William Murphy (b. 15 December 1875 Scotswood, Northumberland – d. 1954 Hoddesdon, Hertfordshire); Mary

Ann Murphy (b. 15 May 1878 Murton Colliery, Co. Durham – alive at 1911 Census – d. unknown).

These three children – and no others – appear in the civilian records (BMD, census, etc.). Murphy's epitaph stated that 'Three of his sons died or were killed in Her Majesty's service' before 1893.

Sacred to the memory of
Michael Murphy
formerly Sgt in the 2nd Battalion
Military Train and the 7th Hussars
who for conspicuous gallantry
during the Indian Mutiny where
he received five serious wounds in saving
the life of a wounded officer
obtained the Victoria Cross
Born in Tipperary – 1832
Died Darlington 4 April 1893
RIP
Three of his sons died or were
killed in Her Majesty's service
This stone is erected to his memory
by his comrades
Sir Henry Havelock Allan Bart

It is known that his son George died in 1954, and that Mary Ann and her family survived into the twentieth century, so his son Edward John Murphy and two further (step)sons must have died before 1893. The army records suggest that these deaths may have been: James Ballard, an alleged stepson of Murphy and a colour sergeant of the 1st Battalion 24th Regiment of Foot who was killed at the Battle of Isandhlwana on 22 January 1879. A sergeant of artillery named Murphy was killed at Tel-el-Kebir on 13 September 1882, and a corporal of the Durham Light Infantry named Murphy died on the Nile in 1885. However the exact identity and fate of all his children are not known; nor is the connection to his niece Bridget Dobson.

NEWELL, Robert
Rank / Service: Private, 9th Lancers (The Queen's Royal)
VC Location: Lord Ashcroft VC Collection
Date of Gazette: 24 December 1858
Place / Date of Birth: Seaham, Co. Durham, 1835
Place / Date of Death: India, 11 July 1858
Grave: Imballa Cemetery, India (grave not marked)
Town / County Connections:

Account of Deed: On 19 March 1858 at Lucknow, India, Private Newell rescued a comrade whose horse had fallen on bad ground, and took him to safety under heavy fire from a large number of the enemy.

Biographical Detail: Newell died four months later of severe diarrhoea at Haryana, India. His Victoria Cross was awarded posthumously.

ROBSON, Henry Howey
Rank/Service: Private, 2nd Bn, Royal Scots (The Lothian Regiment)
VC Location: Royal Scots Museum, Edinburgh
Date of Gazette: 18 February 1915
Place/Date of Birth: South Shields, Co. Durham, 27 May 1894
Place/Date of Death: Toronto, Canada, 4 March 1964
Grave: York Cemetery, Military Section, Toronto, Canada
Town/County Connections: South Shields; Shotton Bridge, Co. Durham

Account of Deed: On 14 December 1914 near Kemmel, France, during an attack on a German position, Private Robson left his trench under very heavy fire and rescued a wounded NCO. Subsequently, during another attack, he tried to bring a second wounded man into cover while exposed to heavy fire. In this attack, he was wounded almost at once, but persevered in his efforts until wounded a second time.

Biographical Detail: Henry Robson VC was among the guests who attended King George V's afternoon garden party held at Buckingham Palace on the 26 June 1920 for recipients of the Victoria Cross.

WAKENSHAW, Adam Herbert
Rank / Service: Private, 9th En, Durham Light Infantry
VC Location: Durham Light Infantry Museum, Durham
Date of Gazette: 11 September 1942
Place / Date of Birth: Newcastle upon Tyne, Northumberland, 9 June 1914
Place / Date of Death: Mersa Matruh, Egypt, 27 June 1942
Grave: El Alamein War Cemetery, Egypt
Town / County Connections: Newcastle upon Tyne, Northumberland

Account of Deed: Tobruk fell to Rommel in hard fighting on 21 June. Before dawn on the 27th his troops encountered the 151st Brigade south of Mersa Matruh, Western Desert. On a rocky plateau known as Point 174 the 9th Battalion Durham Light Infantry had hastily constructed low piles of stone in lieu of foxholes. Four anti-tank guns were positioned ahead on a forward slope, one per company. Private Adam Wakenshaw, aged 28, a very tough Geordie from the Durham coalfields, was among the crews. As the enemy advanced under a full moon, his 2pdr put a round through the engine of a tractor hauling a light gun at 200 yds. A following gun opened up, and Wakenshaw's position came under intense mortar and shell fire, killing or wounding all its gunners.

Wakenshaw lay with his left arm blown off above the elbow. Seeing the enemy attempting to reach their own stranded gun, he crawled back to his 2pdr, where Private Eric Mohn its aimer was also badly wounded. With Wakenshaw as one-armed loader they got off five rounds, a direct hit damaging the light gun and burning its tractor. An incoming shell then killed Mohn and further injured Wakenshaw, who was blown some distance. Unbelievably, he dragged himself back yet again, cradled another round into the breech and was about to fire when a direct hit on the ammunition killed him instantly and wrecked the gun. The three forward rifle companies, which had helplessly watched the drama ahead of them, were progressively overrun and captured. When the enemy withdrew that night, Wakenshaw was buried beside his shattered gun. It now rests in Durham's DLI Museum, an enduring witness of his act of supreme valour. Private Adam Wakenshaw was honoured with a posthumous Victoria Cross.

Biographical Detail: Born in Newcastle upon Tyne on 9 June 1914, he had gone to work at Elswick pit at the age of 14. A pre-war soldier in the Territorial Army, he had been mobilised when war broke out and fought in France in 1940 before being sent with his battalion to North Africa, where he took part in the Battle of Gazala where the British, spread out across the desert in defensive 'boxes', had tried to hold off the German advance. Some recollections of Private Wakenshaw are given below.

Corporal James Wilkinson, 9th Battalion, Durham Light Infantry:

> He was a good soldier in the soldier fashion but he wasn't a smart soldier. He wasn't one of these regimental bods. He was down to earth and you might think he was a little bit slovenly, not a guardsman-type if you know what I mean. We often used to talk, 'cause I think Adam was the same nature as me, really; we got on like a house afire when we saw each other. He was a very nice lad. Quiet. He wasn't very talkative; he was sort of selective, because he thought some people thought themselves better than him. He was a very nice lad. He'd worked in the pits for a bit. I liked Adam.

Private Richard Atkinson, 9th Battalion, Durham Light Infantry:

> He was a smashing bloke. If you were going out at night-time he looked rough and ready and you might go, 'Keep clear, he's a right handful, a rough "un"' – he looked that type. But he was exactly the opposite; he had a heart of gold. If you stayed out, he'd stay sober to make sure you got back. Things like that. He looked after you, he was that type of a lad; if you looked at him you got the completely wrong impression. A nice lad altogether. Oh yes, I knew him well, Wakenshaw. He could look after himself ... handle himself, he could be handy with his fists and things like that, but not vicious, you know what I mean? If there'd been a boxing competition, he'd win it hands down.

Private John Rodgers, 9th Battalion, Durham Light Infantry [for Africa]:

We were in Tiverton to prepare for embarkation. We had all kind of jobs to do, like stencils on kitbags, preparing stores for the embarkation, but we spent a nice time there. We were in a town and out of the field and they used to organise dances at night-time and the company used to organise impromptu concerts. And there's one thing in particular I'd like to mention about Tiverton [Devon]. We had been out for a drink and we'd come out at night-time and we were walking back to the barracks and there were two chaps in front of me and one of them was called Wakenshaw. And we passed some scrimmages going on over by the side of the road, kind of a fight, soldiers were crowded round, and he turned back to go to them. I shouted to him, I said, 'Wack!' – we used to call him 'Wack' for short – 'It's got nothing to do with us, you carry on, man!' He said, 'No, not on your life, that's a Durham in there,' and he walked in and he sorted the whole lot out. I've never seen anything like it in all my life. Scattered the whole crowd. He picked the fella up who was being punched by another fella, put his hat on and just walked him away and put him out in front of him and walked behind him on the way back to the barracks.

He was just a kind of rough diamond type of a lad. He was just a hard man; he had been brought up hard. He used to box for Murphy, the showman, used to go three rounds with him. I think he'd lost a son. We had a long talk when we had a bit of a scheme [an exercise] before we went to Bir Hakeim, I had a long chat to him about his home life, and he was a bit of a lad at school, you know. They used to tell his mother and his mother used to go up and see the teacher; and he said it was his own fault, he'd really been in trouble, but you know how mams and dads are, they try to go and sort the teachers out. And he said, 'I don't even go to church and I see you going when you're having your Mass and I see the lads going and I always want to go. I cannae buck up courage.' I said, 'There's no reason why you shouldn't. I'll go and see the padre and tell him and you'll be OK.' He said, 'Would you?' He was having that feeling that he wanted to attend to his religious duties again. So I took him up to see the padre and the padre said, 'Leave him with me,' and he must have made his peace with God and he come back and he was happy.

A new anti-tank company was formed, it must have taken place in the Gazala Box, and I was then given the job of store man and when this company had been formed some of the soldiers were left over and one of them come to me. It was Adam Wakenshaw. He'd been missed off the gun crew and was surplus to the make-up of the new anti-tank platoon that had formed, so he come to me and he said he'd been posted. He said, 'I've been with the Territorials, in D Company, all the time the war's been going on and I'm going to be sent back now, there's no room for us on the guns.' I said, 'What do you want me to do!' He said, 'You're well in with these people' – the officers – 'can you not see me kept in the battalion?' Major Woods was the Company Commander then and he was a person that you could approach without any worries, so I said, 'Hang on and I'll go and see him,' and I went and saw Major Woods. He said, 'The Company's made up, what do you want me to do!' I said, 'He's out there, he's never been out of D Company, he's nearly in tears. Before we get much further up there somebody's going to go down with sand-fly fever or something like that and you might need somebody else for the gun crew.' So he said, 'Well, can you find him a job!' I said, 'I can find him a job all right'. He said, 'Right, just hang on to him for a bit.'

So poor old Adam Wakenshaw might have been posted, might have been sent away, but he was kept in the battalion. Next time I saw him, he said he'd been taking training for the gun and he was delighted. And I saw him again, later on, after that, and he come and told me especially: he said, 'I'm on the gun crew!' And it was his own doing, he used me as an instrument and Major Woods had to make the decision, but it was his own decision, he wanted to be on the gun, and he was granted it and it worked out that he won the Victoria Cross. But it might have been different. He might have been sent away somewhere else.

And before moving up – we knew we were going up to some kind of action – the C of Es were having a service in one place and the RCs were having another one, 'Abide With Me' was ringing out in the distance, and I saw Adam Wakenshaw coming back from Holy Communion. After that, I never saw him again. That was the last time I saw him. I would say he was just a kind lad, rough and ready. I don't know if he would be the best of soldiers but he'd been in the Territorial Army and that was his life. He wouldn't let anybody down. He proved it to me in the early days when we were at Tiverton. If you were a Durham, that was it. And that was why he was crying, he didn't want to leave the Durhams, he'd been with them all the time. He was wrapped up in the Durham Light Infantry and he thought it was sacrilege that Adam Wakenshaw had to be posted away from it.

Private Richard Atkinson, 9th Battalion, Durham Light Infantry:

We came down to Mersa Matruh, we stopped and they said, 'We're going to make a stand here and get organised.' You could see the coast road and the sea, by this time it was getting dark, and we just sort of stopped on an escarpment, a ridge thing like a hillock. And that's when Wakenshaw won his VC, that night.

Nobody knew what was happening, we'd just sort of stopped, and Adam Wakenshaw was with us with the anti-tank gun and three or four vehicles and some men behind him – I think they must have been mostly transport. And the next thing we knew, this stupid Ned Sparks was shouting in the middle of the night, 'Is that the 9th Transport?' Well, Jerry was about twenty yards behind him and fired at him and hit us. And that's when Wakenshaw started firing back.

By this time it was breaking daylight and Wakenshaw was firing at them. I was lying about ten yards behind Wakenshaw at the time, he had the top of his head off, his arm was away and he was blind and that, and his two mates was dead, and he was just shouting, 'Left a bit!

Right a bit! Up a bit!' and he was firing and he knocked this armoured thing out and this car and that. And then, boof, he got it.

Lance Corporal William Ridley, 9th Battalion, Durham Light Infantry:

I didn't see Wakenshaw but we were getting the flak from the guns and what have you. I went up to one of the officers and I said, 'Could you tell us what's happening, sir?' and he says, very tearfully, 'It looks like the last glorious stand.' I said, 'It's nae good crying about it, like,' and I crawled back.

All of a sudden somebody shouted, 'Every man for himself!' So I gets up and, as I got up, wallop, I got one right in the arm and a spurt of blood about fifteen-foot come out of me arm. I knew at least one artery had gone – as it happened there was two arteries gone – and I thought, 'I've got to stop the blood.' I put the heel of me hand into the hole in me arm and I come off the ridge and Andy Davies, the sergeant, come up and he says, 'What's the matter with you?' I says, 'I've been hit.' He says, 'Well, get on the truck.' I says, 'I daren't leave loose of this, otherwise I'm a dead man. 'So him and another sergeant slung us on to the truck. The driver got in and all he done was set the motor away, got a hold of the wheel and sat on the accelerator, like, and he belted out. Of course he wasn't watching where he was going and hit every hole and trench and every time he hit a trench my arm came away and the poor guy sitting next to us was saturated in blood.

When I was in Cairo hospital, a doctor in the ward came in and he told us the state of the battalion, you know. He also told us that one of our lads had been recommended for a VC. I says, 'What did they call him, like?' He says, 'I just can't remember. It was Wake-something. Wakehall or Wake-something.' I said, 'It wasn't Wakenshaw, was it?' He says, 'Yes, it was.' And that was the first time that I heard Wakenshaw had been recommended for the VC.

Corporal George Lambert, 9th Battalion, Durham Light Infantry:

Somebody had the bright idea of us going back to the wadi at Mersa Matruh. I think the officer's name was Pickering. He'd been in charge of some money, supposed to be around six hundred quid or something, he'd dropped it and buried it and somebody had the bright idea of going back to see if there was a possible chance of finding a needle in a haystack. And when we got there, that's when we came across Adam Wakenshaw.

He hadn't been buried. Well, he was still lying exposed, half, buried, so we buried him and two more lads beside him, just where they were. Course, it knocked all the stuffing out of trying to look for anything. After we'd done that we went back to the battalion and I got a cross made up. Normally numbers were stamped on, transferred, but for that particular cross I got a lad called Dave Walton, who was a sign-writer in the platoon – he was an old TA lad, came from Blaydon or Dunstan – I got him to paint everything on. He put the DLI badge and '9th DLI' and his name all painted on. And we took that back and we put it where he was buried.

YOULL, John Scott

Rank/Service: T/2nd Lieutenant, 1st Bn, Northumberland Fusiliers, attached 11th (S) Battalion

Other Decorations: Italian Silver Medal for Valour

VC Location: Lord Ashcroft VC Collection

Date of Gazette: 25 July 1918

Place/Date of Birth: Thorncroft, Thornley, Co. Durham, 6 June 1897

Place/Date off Death: River Piave, ltaly, 27 October 1918

Grave: Giavera British Cemetery, nr. Treviso, Italy

Town/County Connections: Thornley, Co. Durham

Account of Deed: On 15 June 1918 south-west of Asiago, Italy, 2nd Lieutenant Youll was commanding a patrol that came under heavy enemy fire. Sending his men back to safety, he remained to watch the situation and then, unable to rejoin his company, he reported to a neighbouring unit where he took command of a party of men from different units, holding his position against enemy attack until a machine-gun opened fire behind him. He rushed and captured the gun, killing most of the team and opened fire, inflicting heavy casualties. He then carried out three separate counter-attacks, driving the enemy back each time.

Biographical Detail: 'Jack' Youll was the second son of Richard and Margaret Youll of Thorncroft, Thornley, where he was born on 6 June 1897. He was educated at Thornley Council School and left school aged 15, after which he attended technical classes at Wingate provided by Durham County Council. Following this he became an apprentice electrician at Thornley Colliery. On reaching military age, he volunteered and on 1 July 1916 he became a sapper in the Royal Engineers. After training in England, he was sent to France where he made such a favourable impression that he was recommended for a commission. In June 1917, he returned home to find he was now a 2nd Lieutenant in the Northumberland Fusiliers. Returning to France months later, Youll was mentioned in despatches for his bravery at the Battle of Polygon Wood. Transferred to the front with his battalion, he became the first officer with the Northumberland Fusiliers to win the VC since the Battle of Lucknow more than half a century previously.

In 2005, his home village of Thornley unveiled a memorial in his honour. The four faces of the memorial briefly detail his life, Army career and his Victoria Cross citation.

YOUNG, Thomas
Rank/Service: Private, 9th Battalion, Durham Light Infantry
VC Location: Durham Light Infantry Museum, Durham
Date of Gazette: 4 June 1918
Place/Date of Birth: Boldon, Co. Durham, 28 January 1895
Place/Date of Death: Whickham, Co. Durham, 15 October 1966
Grave: St Patrick's Cemetery, High Span, Co. Durham
Memorials: Statue, Vestibule South Shields Town Hall; High Spen Primary
   School
Town/County Connections: Boldon and High Spen, Co. Durham

Significant Remarks: Real name MORRELL, he enlisted under his mother's
maiden name.

Account of Deed: During the period 25–31 March 1918 at Bucquoy, France,
Private Young, a stretcher bearer, worked unceasingly, evacuating the
wounded from seemingly impossible places. On nine different occasions
he went out in front of the lines in broad daylight, under heavy rifle,
machine-gun and shellfire and brought back wounded to safety. Those too
badly wounded to be moved before dressing he dressed under fire and then
carried them back unaided to the lines. He saved nine lives in this manner.

Biographical Detail: Thomas Young was born Thomas Morrell, at Boldon
Colliery, Co. Durham, on 28 January 1895. Young was his mother's maiden
name, which he appears to have used when he joined the 9th Battalion DLI
at Gateshead in 1914, aged 19 years. At the time of his enlistment, he was
working as a hewer at High Spen, near Blaydon, just one of the thousands
of Durham miners who were to serve in their county regiment during the
First World War. He became stretcher bearer 9-1975 (later 203590) Private
Thomas Young.

   At the time of his VC award, on returning home, Thomas Young was
received as a hero at Saltwell Park in Gateshead. Some local newspapers
reported that 10,000 people were present, others 15,000. All agreed,
however, that it was the largest crowd seen in the park since the Diamond
Jubilee of Queen Victoria over twenty years before. On a raised platform

was the Mayor of Gateshead, the Earl of Durham, as Lord Lieutenant of County Durham, and many other local dignitaries. There was a guard of honour from the 1st Durham County Volunteers, Boy Scouts and Church Lads Brigade, plus the Northumberland Fusiliers band from Fenham Barracks and the Tyneside Fife Band. His family sat proudly below him on the front row. The Earl of Durham presented him with an inscribed watch and silver cigarette case and War Bonds. When the cheering died down and it was his turn to speak he kept it brief.

I am not much of a speaker. There's not a man of the Durham's who wouldn't have done what I did; it was just what any one of them would have done if he could. The thing happened to come my way and I did it. That's all.

In later life Thomas Young was known as the 'Cornfield VC' because he got drunk one night and lost his medals in a cornfield. 'He had the whole village out looking for them,' said a spokesman from the South Shields branch of the Durham Light Infantry Association.

On 26 June 1920 Thomas Young was among the list of guests who attended King George V's afternoon party held at Buckingham Palace for recipients of the Victoria Cross.

At the end of the war, Thomas Young VC returned to his work as a hewer underground at High Spen Colliery. In 1920, he rejoined 9th DLI, as a Sergeant, when the Territorial Battalion reformed but was discharged in 1921. In 1939, he re-enlisted in a National Defence Company. The following year his wife, Rachel, died aged just 45 years. He continued to work as a miner, finally as pithead baths' attendant, until ill health forced him to retire. He then moved from his home in East Street, High Spen, to Chopwell, and then in July 1966, to an old people's home – The Hermitage – at Whickham. He died there on 15 October 1966, aged 71, and was buried in St Patrick's churchyard, High Spen, four days later.

There is a slightly oversized bronze statue of Young commissioned by the DLI created by Welsh sculptor Roger Andrews in the reception vestibule of South Shields Town Hall. In 2004, a special stained-glass window was unveiled in his memory at Gibson Court Medical Centre in Boldon Colliery. A memorial to Thomas Young and William Dobson, another VC recipient from High Spen, was unveiled in July 2007 and can be seen in the grounds of High Spen primary school.

Durham Notes

1. Commissioned by the DLI, a slightly oversized bronze statue by the Welsh sculptor Roger Andrews.
2. Although Annand's award was the first Army VC, by the time it was gazetted VCs had already been won by two Royal Navy officers and two RAF aircrew.
3. References for Annand: Canon W M Lummis VC files, held at the National Army Museum on behalf of the Military Historical Society; David Rissik, *The DLI at War: The History of the Durham Light Infantry 1939–1945* (Durham, 1953); Stephen Shannon, *Beyond Praise: The Durham Light Infantrymen who were awarded the Victoria Cross* (Durham, 1998); Major C Lawton MBE, War Diaries of 2nd Battalion DLI (WO 167/728), Light Infantry Office (Durham), various obituaries and newspaper reports; Roderick Bailey, *Forgotten Voices of the Victoria Cross* (Ebury, 2011).
4. See *Journal of the Victoria Cross Journal* (Mar. 2005).
5. James won the MC when serving with the DLI. He was killed at the Battle of Arras in May 1917. Her eldest son, Thomas, who won the DSO, survived the war.
6. I am grateful to The Lodge of Unity 6003, Stockton Masonic Hall, Wellington Street TS18 1RD for supplying this information.
7. *Strand Magazine*, 1 (1891).
8. The Great Mutiny began at Meerut on Sunday 10 May 1857 when native sepoys refused to handle the new Enfield rifle cartridge, which they believed was coated with pig fat, which both Hindu and Muslim alike would not handle on religious grounds. However, this was only a rumour started by those who were plotting to overthrow the British Raj in India.
9. PRO: WO12/898–909.
10. William Goate is in good company, for Highland Road Cemetery is the resting place for seven other VC recipients: Henry Raby, Nathan Hewett, John Roberts, Hugh Cochrane, William Temple, Hugh Shaw and Israel Harding. There are many other interesting non-military graves including that of Frederick Jane, founder of *Jane's Fighting Ships*.
11. Sources for McKean's biographical details: Canadian War Museum Arch. (Ottawa), file on decorations of G B McKean; General Register Office (Southport); Reg. of Births, Willington, 4 July 1888, NA, RG 150, Acc.1992-93/166, file 436568; *Beaver* (London), 22 Mar. 1919; *Edmonton Journal*, 29 June 1918, 11 Nov 1996; *Lethbridge Herald* (Lethbridge, Alta), 1 Dec. 1926; *Morning Bulletin* (Edmonton, 1 July 1918; *Ottawa Citizen*, 28 Mar. 1979; *Presbyterian and Westminster* (Toronto), 18 July 1918; *The Times* (London), 29 June 1918, 29 Nov. 1926; W A Bishop, *Our Bravest and Best: The Stories of Canada's VC Winners* (Toronto, 1995); *F. H. Varley: A Centennial Exhibition*, compiled Christopher Varley (Edmonton, 1981), 34; *The Register of the Victoria Cross*, rev. edn (Cheltenham, 1988); R C Fetherstonhaugh (ed.), *The Royal Montreal Regiment: 14th Battalion, CEF, 1914–1925* (Montreal, 1927); Peter Varley,

Frederick H. Varley (Toronto, 1983); University of Toronto, Library and Archives Canada/MIKAN 3640361.

12. Army records indicate a date of birth of about 1831–2; and, his gravestone states 1832. However, in later life, Michael Murphy was reasonably inconsistent about his age in civilian records, e.g. 1860 aged 23 (implying DoB = 1837), 1871 aged 40 (implying DoB = 1831), 1881 aged 40 (implying DoB = 1841), 1891 aged 51 (implying DoB = 1840), 1893 aged 53 (implying DoB = 1840), indicating a date of birth of about 1837–40.

13. 1891 UK Census: Blackwell, Darlington, Co. Durham, RG12/2043 f. 61 p. 14. Michael Murphy, blacksmith, aged 51.

14. Epitaph on grave.

15. GRO Register of Marriages: June 1860 2a 107 FARNHAM. Michael Murphy, Farrier 2nd Battalion Military Train, bachelor aged 23, son of Michael Murphy blacksmith deceased = Mary Fox, no occupation, spinster aged 21, daughter of Bernard Fox labourer – on 7 April 1860 at Farnham Register Office.

16. 150th anniversary commemoration.

17. Michael Murphy's VC: extract from *The Annual Register.*

Northumberland Victoria Cross Holders

ALLEN, William Wilson
Rank/Service: Corporal (later Sergeant Instructor of Musketry), 2nd Bn,
   24th Regiment (later the South Wales Borderers)
Other Decorations:
VC Location: South Wales Borderers Museum, Brecon
Date of Gazette: 2 May 1879
Place/Date of Birth: Berwick-on-Tweed, Northumberland c.1844
Place/Date of Death: Monmouth, 12 March 1890
Grave: Monmouth Cemetery
Memorials:
Town/County Connections: Monmouth, South Wales

Account of Deed: On 22 and 23 January 1879 at Rorke's Drift, Natal, South Africa, Corporal Allan and another soldier, F J Hitch VC, kept communication with the hospital open, despite being severely wounded. Their determined conduct enabled the patients to be withdrawn from the hospital, and when incapacitated by their wounds from fighting, they continued, as soon as their wounds were dressed, to serve out ammunition to their comrades during the night.

Biographical Detail: Thought to have been born in Newcastle upon Tyne, he was in fact born in the small village of Belford Moor, Northumberland, possibly in 1844, as in October 1859, he enlisted at York, his age given as 15 and signing his name 'Allan', which is also spelt the same on his gravestone in Monmouth Cemetery. Although only small in stature, being 5' 4" tall, he was no shrinking violet, and he ended up confined in the cells on several occasions between 1860 and 1864. After serving in Mauritius and spending thirteen years in the East, he returned to Brecon in 1864. Two years later, he married a local girl Sarah Ann Reeves, together they had a family of seven children. After acquiring a 2nd Class Certificate of Education with the rank of Corporal, he became an Assistant Schoolmaster in Brecon Barracks – where he was awarded a prize for 'Good Shooting and Judgement of Distance'.

Posted back to his battalion in January 1878, the following month he found himself in South Africa. After serving in the Cape Frontier War, he fought at Rorke's Drift on 22 January 1879 where he received his VC and was wounded in the left shoulder.

As he recovered at Helpmakaar, he wrote to his wife, 'Everything is quiet and we don't expect any fighting till the arrival of troops from home. My dear wife, I trust you will feel too thankful to God for having preserved my life to fret over what might have been a great deal worse. I feel very thankful to God for leaving me in the land of the living.'

Corporal Allen returned to England shortly after. He was awarded his medal by Queen Victoria at Windsor Castle on 9 December 1879.

Allen's arm remained partly disabled, but back in Brecon in 1886, he became Sergeant, Instructor of Musketry to C Company 4th Volunteer Battalion, South Wales Borderers at Monmouth.

In February 1890, a flu epidemic struck the Welsh town of Brecon, and after several weeks of serious illness, Allen died of complications from influenza on 12 March 1890. His death left his family unprovided for, so the Mayor of Monmouth set up a benefit appeal to help them. Although his wife later had to sell his medal, it was eventually returned to the South Wales Borderers Museum in Brecon, along with an inscribed pocket watch, given to the museum by his grandson.

CAIRNS, Hugh

Rank / Service: Sergeant, 46th South Saskatchewan Battalion, Saskatchewan
   Regiment, CEF
Other Decorations: DCM
VC Location: Canadian War Museum, Ottawa, Canada
Date of Gazette: 31 January 1919
Place / Date of Birth: Ashington, Northumberland, 4 December 1896
Place / Date of Death: Valenciennes, France, 2 November 1918
Grave: Auberchicourt British Cemetery, France, Grave Ref I.A.8
Memorials: See *Biographical Detail*
Town / County Connections: Ashington, Northumberland

Account of Deed: On 1 November 1918 at Valenciennes, France, when a
machine-gun opened fire on his platoon, Sergeant Cairns seized a Lewis-
gun and single-handed, in the face of direct fire, rushed the post, killed
the crew of five and captured the gun. Later, after killing twelve of the
enemy and capturing eighteen and two guns, he went with a small party
and, although wounded, he outflanked more field- and machine-guns,
killing many and capturing all the weapons. After consolidation he went
with a battle patrol to exploit Marly and forced sixty to surrender, but was
severely wounded. He later collapsed and died next day.

Biographical Detail: Hugh Cairns was born on 4 December 1896 in
Ashington, Newcastle upon Tyne, to George H. and Elizabeth Dotes
Cairns (née Donkin). He was the third of eleven children who emigrated
as a family to Canada, settling in Saskatoon, Saskatchewan, in May 1911,
aged 14. The Cairns family lived at 713 29th Street West until the year
1913, when they moved a short distance into a larger home at 832 Avenue
G North. He worked as an apprentice plumber and lived with his family
until he enlisted on 2 August 1915 with the 65th Battalion.

   He was an active and highly regarded football player. In 1913, Hugh
led his team, the Christ Church Intermediate Boys Football Club, to
the championship of the Sunday School League. He also played for the

St Thomas church team in 1915 when they won the Saskatoon League Championship.

The earliest memorial to Hugh Cairns was unveiled by the Revd B W Pullinger, of Detroit Michigan on 8 June 1921. The Revd Pullinger had been the chaplain of Sergeant Cairns's regiment in France. Standing nearly 20feet high it consists of a 12foot polished granite base and a 6foot statue of Hugh Cairns in football kit carved in Italian marble in Naples. It was erected by the Saskatoon Football Association and is sited in what is now known as Kiwanis Park, near the University Bridge.

The memorial is reputed to be the only war memorial in the world dedicated to football players, and around the base of the statue are listed the names of the seventy-five Saskatoon footballers who lost their lives in the First World War.

The memorial is used in the logo of the Saskatoon District Soccer Association and a representation appears on the medallions that are awarded annually to individual and team award winners.

On 25 July 1936 on the day preceding the unveiling of the Vimy Memorial, the city of Valenciennes renamed a street – L'Avenue du Sergeant Hugh Cairns – and a suitable plaque was mounted on the wall between the houses at Nos.3 and 5. This was the only instance of this type of honour being bestowed upon an Allied non-commissioned officer by a French city. In 1960, the city of Saskatoon named a street and a school after him and his regiment renamed their new armoury to honour him.

In August 1995, a plaque was erected by the provincial government of Saskatoon in a programme to honour historic people, places and events outside what was thought to be his home. This proved incorrect and it took until February 2005 to relocate the plaque to the correct residence – 832 Avenue G North.

CHICKEN, George Bell
Rank/Service: Civilian volunteer with the Indian Naval Brigade
VC Location: Lord Ashford VC Collection
Date of Gazette: 27 April 1860
Place/Date of Birth: Howden Pans, Northumberland, 2 March 1833
Place/Date of Death: At sea, Bay of Bengal, May 1860
Grave: Monmouth Cemetery
Town/County Connections: Jarrow; Sunderland

Significant Remarks: Chicken's naval VC was the only one to be won on horseback, and his was the last civilian VC awarded under Queen Victoria's 'civilians' warrant of December 1858 (enacted after his deed of bravery for which he was granted his medal). Associated with C G Baker VC.

Account of Deed: On 27 September 1858 at Suhednee, near Peroo, Bengal, Mr Chicken, a civilian, attached himself to a party of mixed troopers of mounted police and cavalry. They routed a force of about 700 mutineers and, in the pursuit that followed, Chicken quickly forged ahead, driving his horse recklessly across the river Nullah and through sugar canes and thick jungle. When he caught up with a party of about twenty armed mutineers, he was quite alone. Chicken at once charged them and killed five with his sword, but was then set upon by the rest, knocked off his horse and badly wounded. He would certainly have been killed had not four native troopers of the 1st Bengal Police and the 3rd Sikh Irregulars galloped up and rescued him.

Biographical Detail: It is stated in numerous official records and documents that George Bell Chicken VC was born in Bishopwearmouth, Co. Durham, in 1838. However, after extensive research by Mr Geoffrey 'Geoff' Matthews, it is now known that George Bell Chicken VC was in fact born the son of George Chicken, master mariner, and Elizabeth (née Bell) of Howden Pans, Northumberland, and was baptised on 8 December 1833 in St Peter's church, Wallsend,[1]

An extract from the book *Local Records* by T Fordyce quotes from an unnamed newspaper of 27 April 1860:

Mr. Chicken is the son of Mr. George Chicken, ship-owner of Jarrow, and brother in law of Mr. James Hamilton, shipbroker of Sunderland. Mr Chicken, eleven years ago (c.1849), before he had attained the age of twenty one, passed a most successful examination and sailed from England as a Chief Officer in a large East Indiaman. He afterwards joined the Indian Navy and soon became sailing master. When the mutiny broke out he joined Peel's Naval Brigade and during the continuance of the struggle his name was frequently mentioned in the Bombay and other journals for his acts of gallantry and daring.

It would appear his parents married at Jarrow c.1825, but by 1851 they were living at Saugh House, East Howden, Wallsend, where it is recorded in the Census that Elizabeth and her family, along with her father, George Bell, farmer of 50 acres, resided.[2] There was no mention of a husband, or son called George, but four daughters (one born in London) and a 4-year-old son called Richard born at Tynemouth in 1846. The absence of father and son was probably due to them being absent on the night of the 1851 Census, and possibly the mention of her father living there might be accounted for as a visit at that date.

The four daughters were named Elizabeth, Mary Ann, Jane and Eliza, all baptised at Wallsend. Mary Ann married James Hamilton, ship broker at Tynemouth in 1853. Eliza married a George Clark, widower, and master mariner, at Shadwell Parish Church, Middlesex, in October 1862, by which date the Chicken family had moved south to Shadwell, London. The witness signatures to the marriage certificate were William Chicken, who may have been a younger brother, and George Chicken, her father, whose address was 35 King David's Lane, Shadwell.

The 4-year-old Richard on the 1851 census, address Saugh House, was actually named Richard Hubback Chicken. On his birth certificate, father George Chicken, master mariner, and mother Elizabeth Bell. The middle name of Hubback was, as is often the case, a family surname on the female side, and incorporated to perpetuate family connections. A Jane Chicken (born c.1803 in South Shields, Durham), married a Michael Hubback at

Jarrow in 1827.[3] Her parents were given as George Chicken, glassmaker, of Gateshead and Elizabeth (née Hindmarch) of Houghton-le-Springs, Co. Durham. Another of their children was named Thomas, who became a surgeon who had moved to Nottingham by 1838 to practise. In the 1851 Census, an Elizabeth Hubback had being staying as a visitor with Thomas and his family in Nottingham, her age given as 7 years old and born in London (c.1844).

George Bell Chicken VC began his maritime career, aged around 14, in the year 1847.[4] He sailed on the *Anna*, registered in Liverpool, as an apprentice for five and a quarter years. His Seamen's Ticket (no. 549720) gave a physical description of him – brown hair and eyes, of dark complexion, with a scar on his right cheek. On 20 February 1852, he received his Mates certificate (Ticket No.3750) at Sunderland.[5] On 24 February 1852, only days after passing his examination, he once again joined the *Anna* at Tynemouth but as second mate, and sailed for the West Coast of America, returning in May 1852. He then voyaged in July 1852 from Hull to Valparaiso, Chile, returning to Shields. In 1853 he made various voyages as 'Only Mate', presumably first mate, on a ship called the *Darlington*, registered in Shields, to Copenhagen and other ports in the Baltic, becoming in 1854 the Captain of that ship on further trips to the Baltic.

His last voyages were two trips to Madras out of Shields and Irvine, Ayrshire, as mate (or possibly master) in the spring of 1855 on a ship called *Hastings*, also registered in Sunderland, and the entries in the Register end by saying 'Disd. 25 July 1855 Calcutta' from the *Hastings*, where he had been temporary acting master. The Register entry stated he had been born at Howden Pans, Northumberland, in 1833, and that he had left the Merchant Service in 1855 in Calcutta, India.

In John Winton's book, *The Victoria Cross at Sea* (1978) there is some information about Chicken's career during the period of the Indian Mutiny.

He enlisted as a Volunteer serving with the Indian Naval Brigade and was appointed into the Service on 31 July 1858, as Acting Master, borne on the books of HMS *Calcutta*. After a few months at Fort William, on the 23 March 1859, he left for Buxar to join No.3 Detachment of the Naval Brigade, serving in the rough broken country and jungles of Jagdispur in Bengal against the mutineers under the brothers Kunwar and Amar Singh, taking with him a party of seamen to replace the sick and dead of No.7 stationed at Dahree.

On 27 September 1858 George Chicken attached himself to a mixed party of the 3rd Sikh Irregular Cavalry and 68 men of Rattray's mounted police, under Lieutenant Charles George Baker of the Bengal Police, on an attack on a force of about 700 mutineers encamped at a village called Suhejnee, near Peroo, in Bengal. Apparently, Chicken had openly announced his determination to win a Victoria Cross and he behaved with conspicuous gallantry during the charge that day. The mutineers were routed and soon in flight, pursued by Chicken and the others … On receiving the despatches of Colonel Turner, in overall command of the cavalry column, Sir Colin Campbell (later Lord Clyde) recommended both Baker and Chicken for the Victoria Cross, and both duly received it.

The *North & South Shields Gazette* newspaper stated: 'Soon after the breaking out of the war he volunteered into the Naval Brigade, and earned for himself distinction under the walls of Delhi, where for his bravery he was promoted to the rank of Master I.N.'[6]

There is a further interesting (undated and unattributed) note in his Imperial War Museum files: 'Joined the Indian Navy and was one of the Indian Naval Brigade during the Mutiny in 1857–58. Was present at action where the Brigade shelled the mutineers from their position in Fort Kali Kanki: also at operations in Jagdispur.'[7]

The Indian Mutiny was finally quelled in April 1859. He never saw or handled his VC – although gazetted on 27 April 1860. George Bell Chicken returned to HMS *Calcutta* on 30 November 1859, and in March 1860 was given command of HM Schooner *Emily* (2 guns), which was subsequently lost at sea with all hands in a violent squall off Sandheads in the Bay of Bengal in May 1860. It is reported that the medal was posted by Sir Edward

Lugard to his father, George Chicken, master mariner, at 35 King David Lane, Shadwell, East London, on 4 March 1862.[8] King David Lane still exists, though there are no remaining original dwellings – only a school on one side and council flats and industrial units on the other. A search of the 1841 Census in this area found an entry for his parents at the Coal Meters Arms, Lower Shadwell, where his grandmother Elizabeth Chicken (née Hindmarch: the brewer's daughter) was the landlady.

Chicken's was the only naval VC to be won on horseback! It was also the last civilian VC awarded, under Queen Victoria's 'civilians' warrant of December 1858 (enacted incidentally AFTER his Deed of Bravery for which he was granted the medal).[9]

Lastly, on the subject of Chicken's Victoria Cross medal. On 26 October 2006 George Chicken's medals were sold at auction by Moreton & Eden. The lot comprised of his Indian Mutiny Medal (1857–8) and his VC medal inscribed on the reverse 'Mr G B Chicken, Indian Navy. Septr 4th 1858'. This was believed to be the original VC prepared and forwarded to India for presentation to George Chicken before his death had become known by the War Office. After Chicken's untimely death in May 1860 the Cross should have been returned to England, but appears to have been either lost or retained in India. This particular Chicken Victoria Cross now has the unusual status of being an original but unawarded VC, while a duplicate but official Victoria Cross was duly presented to George Chicken's father in 1862.[10]

The Victoria Cross was purchased for £48,000 on behalf of the Michael Ashcroft Trust, the holding institution for Lord Ashcroft's VC Collection.

This auction by Morton & Eden was the second day's sale of the whole of the American Numismatic Society's Medal Collection. A major donor of medals to the ANS. was John Sandford Saltus, but the exact date of his acquisition of the Chicken Victoria Cross is unknown, but it must have been before 1922 when he died.

Interestingly, in 1932 Messrs A H Baldwin & Sons of London are known to have handed another VC to George Chicken, together with personal correspondence and related items indicating a firm provenance to the

Chicken family. The Cross and associated items were sold privately to a collector and resurfaced at an auction in 1987 in Red Deer, Alberta, Canada, and the box still contained a letter about the award; again it was sold to an anonymous buyer. This Victoria Cross is unavailable for inspection so a direct comparison with the American Numismatic Society Cross is not possible.

Finally, to make matters even more confusing, a further Victoria Cross named to George Chicken is known to exist in private hands, although the engraving on this VC appears to place it in the category of a 'copy' produced for an unknown reason.

No photographs of the man himself have ever been located.

DOBSON, Frederick William
Rank/Service: Private (later Corporal), 2nd Bn Coldstream Guards
VC Location: Coldstream Guards RHQ, Wellington Barracks
Date of Gazette: 9 December 1914
Place/Date of Birth: Ovingham, Northumberland, 19 November 1886
Place/Date of Death: Newcastle upon Tyne, 15 November 1935
Grave: Ryton & Crawcrook Cemetery, Co. Durham – Section A, Plot 234
Memorials: High Spen Primary School, Co. Durham
Town/County Connections: Ovingham, Wallsend

Account of Deed: Near the French village of Chavanne Dobson was one of half a dozen volunteers who offered to move a barricade erected over a canal by the Germans. In what was to be known as the Battle of the Aisne both sides, finding progress impossible, began to dig themselves trenches and settle in to a protracted conflict.

The morning of 28 September 1914 was very misty. Three men of Dobson's battalion had been sent out on patrol duty, and when the haze cleared found themselves in the open about 150 yards from the German trenches. The Germans opened a heavy fire. One of the patrol was successful in regaining the British trench, although he was hit in the arms and received five bullets in one leg. Unfortunately his comrades fared worse. One man was struck down at once, while the other's bold dash for life was soon checked and he, too, was hit and fell. Captain Follett saw what had happened to his men, and called for a volunteer to go out and bring in the wounded men who were lying helpless in the open.

Dobson without hesitation volunteered and left the safety of his trench for what appeared to be certain death, as the Germans continued their heavy fire. He showed no fear, however, but coolly crept over the parapet and crawled through the mangels in the field in front. He got safely through this field, but when he reached the open and raised his head to take his bearings the Germans saw him and fired. This warning made him cautious, and he 'ducked' his head, but not before he had noticed the exact spot where one of the patrol was lying. How to reach the man was the problem that now presented itself, for every time that Dobson raised his head the

Germans poured a volley of bullets in his direction. Dobson soon realised however, that if he did not reach the fallen man quickly he would bleed to death, so he concluded that his best plan was to lie still on the ground in order to induce the enemy to believe that he was dead – struck by one of their bullets – and then to make a dash.

It was a hazardous proceeding, but fortunately the plan succeeded, for as long as Dobson lay still on the ground no further shots were fired. After several minutes' rest Dobson, having nerved himself for the great undertaking, leapt to his feet and making a desperate dash succeeded in reaching his man. He was shocked, however, to find that the poor fellow was past human aid. Of the two men who had been struck down he had missed the wounded and risked his life for the dead. The former was lying nearer the British trenches and had not been seen by Dobson. Before leaving the fallen soldier, Dobson took as many particulars as he could from his papers, etc. He tried to get possession of his rifle but could not, as the dead man was lying on it, and to raise him up would have been to court death from the vigilant Germans: thus Dobson crawled back with his head toward the enemy as this lessened the target; but he received a bullet through his heel.

When he reached the mangel field Dobson waved his hand to let his comrades know he was safe. They saw the signal and risked raising their heads. They peered at him over the parapet, and encouraged him to make the final spurt to safety. Climbing over the parapet as coolly as if he had just returned from a stroll, Dobson went at once to his Major and reported what he had done, giving the name and other particulars of the dead soldier.

The officer listened to Dobson's report, and then asked what had happened to the other man, and it was not till then that Dobson realised that two of his comrades had been lying in the open. Turning to his officer Dobson very quietly said that he would go out again and endeavour to bring in the stricken man. The officer, struck with the guardsman's superb gallantry, decided that he would do all he could to make the journey as safe as possible. He gleaned from Dobson some important particulars about the range of the German guns, and then arranged for the British artillery to fire upon the German positions.

Private Dobson adopted exactly the same plan as before when he proceeded on his second life-saving exploit. Creeping out of the trench, he crawled cautiously among the mangels, taking every care to conceal his movements from the Germans. He peered around and at length discovered the exact place where the wounded man lay. Then he braced himself for the final spurt and succeeded in wriggling his way to the stricken soldier. In dragging the man to the British trench Dobson had the assistance of Corporal Brown, who, he says, 'was brave, and never showed the least fear'. This generous tribute is characteristic of Dobson. Corporal Brown was awarded the Distinguished Conduct Medal, but did not live to hear of this honour, for he died three days before it was officially announced.

Biographical Detail: Frederick William Dobson was born in the pit village of Ovingham, in Northumberland, where, after a rudimentary education, he worked at Garesfield Colliery as a horsekeeper and lodged for a while with a Mr Tommy Broughton at Hookergate; he then lived above Cumberledge's shop in Front Street. Tiring of his occupation, Dobson enlisted as a regular soldier in 1906, and served for three years in the 1st Battalion Coldstream Guards. After three years he returned to his former occupation, taking employment at Backworth Colliery, near Whitley.

At the outbreak of the Great War Corporal Dobson rejoined his old regiment, and was attached to the 2nd Battalion, with which unit he proceeded to France. He landed at Le Havre on 13 August 1914, and from the first saw service as his battalion was one of many units that composed the original British Expeditionary Force (BEF).

After his exploits at Aisne, Dobson fought in several other conflicts, including the first Battle of Ypres where he was badly wounded and mentioned in despatches. About this time he actually had a spell of twenty-three days in the trenches without being relieved. He was present at Festubert, La Bassée and Givenchy where he was again wounded when helping to make a dugout, and was invalided home in December 1914.

When it became known that he was in London, King George V expressed his desire to present the Victoria Cross himself. There ensued a search to find Dobson: as an officer put it, 'We just managed to catch him' as he prepared to travel North. Corporal Dobson, who was in mufti, was hurried off to the regimental headquarters, supplied with full-dress uniform, and conducted to Buckingham Palace accompanied by two officers of the Coldstream Guards.

After he left the army, in 1935 Frederick Dobson was living in rented rooms at Westgate, Newcastle upon Tyne. Taken ill, he was admitted to the city hospital on 13 November, where he died aged 49 years of age. It is said that his wounds had troubled him for the rest of his life. While feted during his military career, after demobilisation he had found it difficult to get regular work because of his wounds and he became embittered and disillusioned.

He was buried with full military honours in Ryton Cemetery, Co. Durham. For fifty years, however, Dobson's grave lay unattended and obscured by undergrowth until the local branch of the Coldstream Guards Association was alerted to its plight. On 15 March 1986 the Association held a service of thanksgiving at the graveside and dedicated a new headstone. In 2014 the Newcastle upon Tyne branch of the Coldstream Guards Association took formal ownership of the plot, ensuring that it will be looked after in perpetuity; at the same time it was refurbished and kerbing added to the grave.

By way of postscript, in 1936, Dobson's medals turned up in a pawnbroker's shop in Newcastle and the Coldstream Guards took possession and they are now in the Regimental Museum.

JENNINGS, Edward

Rank/Service: Rough Rider, Bengal Artillery
Other Decorations:
VC Location: 'F' Battery, Royal Artillery
Date of Gazette: 24 December 1858.
Place/Date of Birth: Ballinrobe, Co. Mayo, Ireland, 1815
Place/Date of Death: North Shields, Northumberland, 10 May 1889
Grave: Heaton Cemetery, Newcastle upon Tyne (erected 1999)
Memorials: Preston Cemetery, North Shields
Town/County Connections: Ballinrobe, Co. Mayo; North Shields

Account of Deed: During the whole of the period 14 to 22 November 1857, at the Relief of Lucknow, India, Rough Rider Jennings acted with conspicuous gallantry (elected by the regiment under rule 13 of the royal warrant).

Biographical Detail: After retirement from the Army, Jennings worked as a Corporation labourer at North Shields.

JOHNSON, James Bulmer
Rank/Service: 2nd Lieutenant, 2nd Bn, Northumberland Fusiliers, attd 36th Battalion
Other Decorations:
VC Location: Northumberland Fusiliers Museum, Alnwick Castle
Date of Gazette: 26 December 1918
Place/Date of Birth: Widdrington, Northumberland, 31 December 1889
Place/Date of Death: Plymouth, Devon, 23 March 1943
Grave: Efford Crematorium, Plymouth
Memorials:
Town/County Connections: Bedlington, Northumberland; Plymouth, Devon

Account of Deed: On 14 October 1918 south-west of Wez Macquart, France, during operations by strong patrols, 2nd Lieutenant Johnson repelled frequent counter-attacks and for six hours, under heavy fire, he held back the enemy. When at length he was ordered to retire Johnson was the last to leave the advanced position carrying a wounded man. Three times subsequently 2nd Lieutenant Johnson returned and brought in badly wounded men under intense enemy machine-gun fire.

Biographical Detail: According to the corporal who brought him the telegram informing him that he was to receive the VC, 'When I gave it to the officer, he read, waltzed me round his billet and then threw every bit of his shaving kit through the window.'

LAIDLAW, Daniel Logan
Rank/Service: 15851 Piper (later Sergeant-Piper), 7th Battalion, King's Own Scottish Borderers
Other Decorations:
VC Location: National War Museum of Scotland, Edinburgh
Date of Gazette: 18 November 1915
Place/Date of Birth: Little Swinton, near Berwick-upon-Tweed, Northumberland, 26 July 1875
Place/Date of Death: Shoresdean, Berwick-upon-Tweed, 2 June 1950
Grave: St Cuthbert's Church, Norham, Northumberland (2002)
Memorials:
Town/County Connections: Little Swinton and Shoresdean, near Berwick-upon-Tweed, Northumberland

Significant Remarks: Known as the 'Piper of Loos'.

Account of Deed: On 25 September 1915 near Loos and Hill 70, France, prior to an assault on enemy trenches and during the worst of the bombardment, Piper Laidlaw, seeing that his company was shaken with the effects of gas, with complete disregard for danger, mounted the parapet and, marching up and down, played his company out of the trench. The effect of his splendid example was immediate and the company dashed to the assault. Piper Laidlaw continued playing his pipes even after he was wounded and until the position was won.

Biographical Detail: Born in 1875 in Little Swinton, Berwickshire, Daniel Laidlaw joined the 2nd Battalion, Durham Light Infantry on 11 April 1896 where he was immediately posted to India where he stayed for two years until June 1898. Whilst there he was employed on plague duty in Bombay from March to May 1898. After returning to Britain, he was claimed out of the DLI by his eldest brother and served in the King's Own Scottish Borderers as a piper until April 1912, when he was placed on the reserve.

Upon the outbreak of war in Europe, Daniel Laidlaw re-enlisted in his old regiment on 1 September 1914 and went to France with the regiment the following June. Daniel Laidlaw was promoted to sergeant-piper on

12 October 1917, and was eventually demobilised on 3 April 1919; total service 20 years 6 months.

He died peacefully in 1950, aged 74, at Shoresedean, near Norham, Northumberland, and was buried in St Cuthbert's churchyard. There is also a memorial plaque within the church. A ceremony took place at St Cuthbert's churchyard, on 2 June 2002 to place a headstone over the grave of Piper Daniel Laidlaw VC, 'The Piper of Loos'. The project was organised by the King's Own Scottish Borderer's Museum in Berwick-on-Tweed and by members of the Laidlaw family.

Piper Laidlaw left an account of his VC action in his own words:

On Saturday morning we got orders to raid the German trenches. At 6.30 the bugles sounded the advance and I got over the parapet with Lieutenant Young. I at once got the pipes going and the laddies gave a cheer as they started off for the enemy's lines. As soon as they showed themselves over the trench top they began to fall fast, but they never wavered, but dashed straight on as I played the old air they all knew 'Blue Bonnets over the Border'. I ran forward with them piping for all I knew, and just as we were getting near the German lines I was wounded by shrapnel in the left ankle and leg. I was too excited to feel the pain just then, but scrambled along as best I could. I changed my tune to 'The Standard on the Braes o' Mar', a grand tune for charging on. I kept on piping and piping and hobbling after the laddies until I could go no farther, and then seeing that the boys had won the position I began to get back as best I could to our own trenches.

LAWSON, Edward

Rank / Service: Private, 1st Battalion, Gordon Highlanders
Other Decorations:
VC Location: Gordon Highlanders Museum, Aberdeen
Date of Gazette: 20 May 1898
Place / Date of Birth: Newcastle upon Tyne, Northumberland, 11 April
   1873
Place / Date of Death: Walker, Northumberland, 2 July 1955
Grave: Heaton Cemetery, Newcastle upon Tyne (erected 1999)
Memorials:
Town / County Connections: Newcastle upon Tyne and Walker, Northumberland

Account of Deed: On 20 October 1897, during the attack on the Dargai
Heights, North-West Indian Frontier (Tirah Campaign), Private Lawson
carried a Lieutenant of the Gordon Highlanders, who was severely
wounded, out of a heavy fire. Subsequently, although wounded himself, he
returned and brought in another casualty.

Biographical Detail:

LEACH, James
Rank/Service: 2nd Lieutenant (later Captain), 2nd Bn, Manchester Regt
Other Decorations:
VC Location: Private (not on public display)
Date of Gazette: 22 December 1914
Place/Date of Birth: North Shields, Northumberland, 27 July 1892
Place/Date of Death: Shepherd's Bush, London, 15 August 1958
Grave: Mortlake Crematorium
Memorials:
Town/County Connections: North Shields; London

Account of Deed: On 29 October 1914 near Festubert, France, after
the enemy had taken their trench and two attempts to recapture it had
failed, 2nd Lieutenant Leach and Sergeant J Hogan VC with a party of
ten volunteers went to recover it themselves. They took the Germans by
surprise with a sudden bayonet attack and then, working from traverse to
traverse, they gradually succeeded in regaining possession, killing eight of
the enemy, wounding two and taking sixteen prisoners.

Biographical Detail:

LIDDELL, John Aiden
Rank/Service: Captain, 3rd Bn, Argyll and Sutherland Highlanders (Princess Louise's) and Royal Flying Corps
Other Decorations: MC (gazetted 18 February 1915)
VC Location: Lord Ashcroft VC Collection
Date of Gazette: 23 August 1915
Place/Date of Birth: Newcastle upon Tyne, Northumberland, 3 August 1888
Place/Date of Death: La Panne, Flanders, 31 August 1915
Grave: Sherfield-on-Lodden church, Hampshire
Memorials: Basingstoke Old Cemetery, Hampshire; RC Church of St Joseph, Pickering
Town/County Connections: Newcastle upon Tyne, Northumberland; Sherfield-on-Lodden, Hants.

Account of Deed: On 31 July 1915, while on flying reconnaissance over Ostend-Bruges-Ghent, Captain Liddell was severely wounded in his right thigh. This caused momentary unconsciousness, but by great effort he recovered partial control of his machine when it had dropped nearly 3,000 feet, and succeeded, although fired on, in completing the course and brought the plane back into Allied lines. The control wheel and throttle control were smashed and also part of the undercarriage and cockpit, but the machine and the life of the Observer 2nd Lieutenant R H Peck were saved. Captain Liddell died a month later.

Biographical Detail: Born on 3 August 1888 at Benwell Hall, Newcastle upon Tyne, John Aidan Liddell was the son of Emily Catherine Liddell and John Liddell KCSG, JP for Northumberland, the eldest boy of three brothers and a sister. Considered in delicate health, he showed early signs of natural talents and gifted insight in many scientific and mechanical subjects. Educated at Stonyhurst College, Lancashire, from September 1900 to 1908, he then entered Balliol College, Oxford.

Among his interests was astronomy, which led to his election in February 1907 to the membership of the British Astronomical Society. At Balliol he undertook the Honours course in zoology and was the only scholar of his year to secure a first-class degree in this subject.

On leaving Oxford Liddell was offered a travelling scholarship to investigate the fauna of the island of Krakatoa (devastated by a volcanic eruption in 1883), but he turned it down in favour of joining the special reserve of officers in the 3rd Battalion, Argyll and Sutherland Highlanders on 1 June 1912. Having an interest in aviation he gained air experience in 1913, eventually undertook private tuition at the Vickers Flying School at Brooklands, and gained his Royal Aero Club Certificate, No. 781, on 14 May 1914.

Promoted to Lieutenant in July 1914, Liddell was further promoted to Captain on the outbreak of war; and on 28 August 1914 he sailed to France with his regiment, with overall responsibility for the machine-gun sections of his battalion. From September 1914 to February 1915, he saw continuous action in the trenches; serving at one period for forty-three consecutive days and nights in the front-line trenches without even a change of clothing!

Liddell's courage and devotion to duty were officially recognised by a mention in despatches, and the award of the Military Cross on 14 January 1915. In February of that year, he returned to England on sick leave suffering from 'battle fatigue'.

After an extended period of recuperation, Liddell transferred to the Royal Flying Corps (RFC), and in May 1915, he was seconded from his regiment, on probation, to the flying service. A period of instruction took place at Shoreham, Dover, and Farnborough, and on 20 July 1915 he was officially transferred to the RFC. Three days later, he returned to France and reported to No. 7 Squadron at St Omer, where he was allotted to A Flight of that unit.

On 29 July 1915 Liddell flew his first operational patrol – a reconnaissance over Ostend-Bruges-Ghent-Audenarde-Heesteert in RE5 2458. Two days later Liddell on 31 July, Liddell undertook his second and fatal sortie in RE5 2457 during which patrol his actions led to the award of his VC.

Liddell languished in hospital for four weeks after receiving wounds on 31 July, resulting in amputation of his right leg and he died on the feast day of St Aidan, 31 August 1915. With him in his last hours was his mother. His body was conveyed to London on 3 September, and on the following day, he was interred in the Roman Catholic section of Basingstoke Old Cemetery, Hampshire.

The award of his Victoria Cross was notified to him personally on 18 August 1915, the actual medal was presented to his father John Liddell JP by King George V at Buckingham Palace on 16 November 1916. His father also paid towards a font in the RC church of St Joseph, Pickering, designed by the renowned artist Eric Gill, as a memorial.

PERCY, Henry Hugh Manvers
Rank / Service: General, 89th (The Princess Victoria's) Regiment of Foot
Other Decorations: KCB, Légion d'Honneur, Order of the Medjidie
VC Location:
Date of Gazette: 5 May 1857
Place / Date of Birth: Cobham, Surrey, 22 August 1817
Place / Date of Death: Eaton Square, Belgravia, 3 December 1877
Grave: Westminster Abbey, London
Memorials: Percy family vault in St Nicholas' chapel, Westminster Abbey
Town / County Connections: Cobham, Surrey; London; Alnwick Castle

Account of Deed: At the Battle of Inkerman on 5 November 1854 at a moment when the Guards were some distance from the Sandbag Battery, Colonel Percy charged singly into the battery, followed immediately by the Guards; the embrasures of the battery, as also the parapet, were held by the Russians who kept up a most severe fire of musketry. Colonel Percy then found himself with many men of various regiments who had charged too far, nearly surrounded by the Russians, and without ammunition. Colonel Percy, by his knowledge of the ground, although wounded, extricated these men and, passing under a heavy fire from the Russians then in the Sandbag Battery, brought them safe to where ammunition was to be obtained, thereby saving some fifty men and enabling them to renew the combat. He received the approval of HRH the Duke of Cambridge for this action on the spot. Percy himself suffered during the action a black eye, gashes to the face and severe contusion on the back of the head. Forty-four members of his company were killed or wounded in the encounter.[11]

Biographical Details: The Hon. Henry Percy, fourth child and third son of George Percy, Lord Lovaine (later 2nd Earl of Beverley) by Louisa Harcourt Stuart-Wortley, third daughter of The Hon. James Stuart-Wortley-Mackenzie, was born at Burwood House, Cobham, Surrey, on 22 August 1817, and educated at Eton. Styled Lord Henry Percy from 1865 after his father became 5th Duke of Northumberland at the age of 86. He entered the British Army as an ensign in the Grenadier Guards on 1 July

1836, and was present during the insurrection in Canada in 1838. Aged 37, he served as a Captain and Lieutenant Colonel in the 3rd Battalion, Grenadier Guards, during the Crimean War of 1854–5. He was present at the Battle of Alma (where he was shot through the right arm), the Battle of Balaklava, the Battle of Inkerman (where he was again wounded) and the Siege of Sebastopol.

On Boxing Day 1854, Percy was taken ill with dysentery and Crimean Fever. He was therefore evacuated to the General Hospital, Scutari, the following month. He survived the very high death rates which were prevalent in the hospitals of Scutari that winter and by mid–February 1855 was well enough to be invalided back to England. He returned voluntarily to the Crimea in May and rejoined his regiment in the trenches before Sebastopol.

He was promoted to full colonel in the summer of 1855, and then held the local rank of Brigadier General in command of the British–Italian Legion in Turin, where he arrived in August. The British–Italian Legion was a mercenary force raised following the passage of the 1854 Foreign Enlistment Act to fight for the Allies (France, Great Britain and Turkey) in the Crimean War, modelled along the lines of similar foreign legions raised in the Napoleonic Wars. The Kingdom of Sardinia had already entered the Crimean War on the side of the Allies and Count Cavour, Prime Minister of Sardinia, was in theory supportive of the British Government and Percy's efforts to recruit and train a fighting force in Turin. However, the project became mired in bureaucracy, suffered from lack of funds and inadequate resources, and was eventually rendered redundant by the fall of Sebastopol in September 1855 and a formal end to hostilities six months later. Percy resigned his command of the British–Italian Legion in October 1855 in a state of total exasperation.[12]

After leaving the British–Italian Legion, Colonel Percy was asked by Lord Stratford de Redcliffe, British Ambassador to Turkey, to attempt to relieve the Siege of Kars, Armenia, which was being defended by Brigadier General Williams. However, Kars fell to the Russians on 28 November

1855, the day after Percy arrived in Constantinople, so the expedition was called off before it got under way.[13]

Colonel Percy was an accomplished linguist and Turkophile, so in January 1856, after the armistice in the Crimea but before the signing of the Treaty of Paris in March 1856, he was ordered by General Codrington, Commander-in-Chief of the British Army in the Crimea, to reconnoitre possible landing places in Asia Minor in case of a continuation of hostilities along the Caucasus front.[14]

From 29 June 1855 he was an aide-de-camp to the Queen – a post he held until 10 February 1865. He was gazetted for the Victoria Cross (VC) on 5 May 1857. As the most senior officer in the British Army to be awarded the VC during the Crimean War, Percy was on the occasion of the first investiture of the Victoria Cross in Hyde Park, London, on 26 June 1857 tasked with commanding the sixty-two recipients who had the decoration pinned to their breasts by Queen Victoria that day.[15]

In the summer of 1861, as commanding officer at the Curragh, he was tasked with overseeing the Prince of Wales's military induction. Colonel Percy was well regarded by the royal family: Prince Albert had previously recommended that Percy's infantry manual, *Brigade Movements* (1853) be distributed to every officer in the Brigade of Guards. In spite of the young prince not being given as much commendation or responsibility in matters of drill as he had hoped, he liked Percy 'very much' – perhaps because the latter, being a strict disciplinarian, insisted on treating him just like any other junior officer. However, the Curragh visit was marred by the Prince's 'fall', following which Queen Victoria blamed her son for Prince Albert's death. 'The fall' came in the form of initiation in carnal pleasure with the actress Nellie Clifden, as arranged by junior officers at the Curragh.[16]

On the occurrence of the Trent Affair in December 1861, Percy was sent to New Brunswick in command of the first battalion of the Grenadier Guards. He had been promoted to Major in 1860, but retired from active service on 3 October 1862 owing to the chronic ill health he had suffered ever since the Crimean War. However, he remained on half-pay and briefly commanded a brigade at Aldershot – the place to which he and another

Grenadier officer, Col. F. W. Hamilton, had first brought the Army in 1853 when they selected Aldershot Heath and its surrounding area as a new training ground.[17]

In 1870, during the Franco-Prussian War, he was sent by HRH the Duke of Cambridge, Commander-in-Chief, as an observer with the Prussian Army at Sedan.[18] On 24 May 1873 he was gazetted a KCB. He was also rewarded for his military services by being appointed to the colonelcy of the 89th (The Princess Victoria's) Regiment of Foot on 28 May 1874. He became a full General on 1 October 1877.

He succeeded his brother, Lord Lovaine, as Conservative Member of Parliament (MP) for Northumberland North from 1865 to 1868. He was found dead in his bed at his residence, 40 Eaton Square, London, on 3 December 1877, and was buried in the Percy family vault in St Nicholas' chapel, Westminster Abbey on 7 December.[19] He never married.

Northumberland Notes

1. Parish Register for Baptisms at St Peter's Church, Wallsend, Northumberland
2. 1851 Census East Howden, Northumberland: HO 107/2409, folio 236.
3. 1851 Census St Paul, Shadwell, Tower Hamlets, Middlesex: HO 107/1550, folio 403v.
4. John Winton, *The Victoria Cross at Sea* (Michael Joseph, 1978); 1851 Census St Paul, Shadwell, Tower Hamlets, Middlesex: HO 107/1550, folio 403v.
5. 'Register of Competency of Masters & Mates', BT122/4 (PRO Kew); National Maritime Museum, Maritime Information Centre, Greenwich, London SE10 9NF. George Bell Chicken became a registered master just about the time that the Registrar General of Shipping & Seamen was compiling an alphabetical register of ship's masters and introducing compulsory examinations for Certificates of Competency for Mates and Masters which took place between 1845 and 1854, a period that covered the 'very successful examination' which George B Chicken supposedly passed around 1849, presumably for his Competency Certificate.
6. *London Gazette,* 27 Apr. 1860.
7. Imperial War Museum, Department of Documents: George Bell Chicken's Victoria Cross File; E M O'Moore Creagh and M Humphris, *The V.C. & D.S.O* (Standard Art Book Co., 1924).
8. M J Crook, *The Evolution of the Victoria Cross* (Midas Books, 1975).
9. Ibid.
10. Ibid.
11. *London Gazette*, 7 May 1857.
12. C C Bayley, *Mercenaries for the Crimea* (McGill-Queen's University Press, 1977).
13. Algernon Percy, *A Bearskin's Crimea: Colonel Henry Percy VC and his Brother Officers* (Leo Cooper, 2005).
14. F W Hamilton, *The Origin and History of the First or Grenadier Guards* (John Murray, 1874).
15. Percy, *A Bearskin's Crimea.*
16. Jane Ridley, *Bertie: A Life of Edward VII* (Chatto & Windus, 2012).
17. Hamilton, *Grenadier Guards.*
18. Percy, *A Bearskin's Crimea.*
19. *Morning Post,* 5 Dec. 1877.

Glossary

Orders and Decorations

BEM	British Empire Medal
CBE	Companion of the Order of the British Empire
CD	Canadian Forces Decoration
CGM	Conspicuous Gallantry MedalCMG Companion of the Most Distinguished Order of St Michael and St George
CVO	Companion of the Royal Victorian Order
DCM	Distinguished Conduct Medal
DFC	Distinguished Flying Cross
DFM	Distinguished Flying Medal
DSC	Distinguished Service Cross
DSM	Distinguished Service Medal
DSO	Distinguished Service Order
GCB	Knight Grand Cross of the Most Honourable Order of the Bath
GCMG	Knight Grand Cross of the Most Distinguished Order St Michael and St George
GCVO	Knight Grand Cross of the Royal Victorian Order
KBE	Knight Commander of the Order of the British Empire
KCB	Knight Commander of the Most Honourable Order of the Bath
KCMG	Knight Commander of the Most Distinguished Order of St Michael and St George
KCVO	Knight Commander of the Royal Victorian Order
MBE	Member of the British Empire
MC	Military Cross
MM	Military Medal
OBE	Order of the British Empire

OM	Order of Merit
RD	Reserve Decoration
VD	Volunteer Decoration

Acronyms and Specialist Terms

Adjutant	The CO's personal staff officer in a battalion or regiment in the British and Indian Armies. In the Second World War, and for several years thereafter, there was no operations officer at this level, so the adjutant was responsible for all operational staff work as well as discipline and all other personnel matters
Aide-de-camp	a general officer's personal assistant; civilian equivalent PA
AIF	Australian Imperial Forces
AMF	Australian Military Forces
ARP	Air Raid Precautions
AWOL	Absent Without Leave
Bde	Brigade
BEF	British Expeditionary Force
Bn	Battalion
Bren	The British light machine gun of the Second World War and until the late 1950s. Fired a standard .303-inch round from a 30-round magazine (usually loaded with 28 rounds)
Brigade	A formation of two or more infantry battalions or armoured regiments, commanded by a brigadier
Brigade Major	The senior operations officer of a brigade, de facto chief of staff
CEF	Canadian Expeditionary Force
Colour Sergeant	The senior sergeant of an infantry company (cf. staff sergeant)
Commando	Can refer to the individual commando soldier or marine, or to the unit. A commando unit was around 450 strong,

	divided into five rifle troops each of about 60 men, a support troop of Vickers medium machine-guns and 3-inch mortars and a head-quarters troop.
Corps	A formation of at least two divisions commanded by a Lieutenant General. Also a generic term for arms and services except armour, artillery and infantry, hence Corps of Royal Engineers, Royal Signals, Royal Army Service Corps, Indian Army Service Corps, Royal Army Medical Corps, Indian Army Medical Corps and so on.
CSM	Company Sergeant Major
DCM	Distinguished Conduct Medal
Division	A formation of two or more brigades commanded by a Major General
Flak	German for anti-aircraft fire, from the German for anti-aircraft gun *flierger-abwehrkanone*, later adopted by all sides and, because it could not readily be spoken by British soldiers, was reduced to the slang term
F/O	Flying Officer
GHQ	General Headquarters
GRO	General Routine Order
GSO	General Staff Officer, a staff officer who dealt with General (G) Staff matters (operations, intelligence, planning and staff duties), as opposed to personnel (A short for Adjutant General's Staff), or logistic matters (Q short for Quartermaster General's Staff). The grades were GSO 1 (Lieutenant Colonel), GSO 2 (Major), and GSO 3 (Captain). The GSO 1 in a division was the senior operations staff officer, effectively the chief of staff. The AAG, or Assistant Adjutant General in a division was the senior personnel staff officer, and the AQMG, or Assistant Quartermaster General, in a division was the senior logistics staff officer

Jerry	Derogatory term used during the period to describe Germans
KRRC	King's Royal Rifle Corps
MO	Medical Officer
MT	Motor Transport
NCO	Non-Commissioned Officer; Lance Corporal to Colour Sergeant
PlAT	Projectile Infantry Anti-Tank: British shoulder-fired weapon issued from mid-1942, effective up to 100 yards, consisting of a tube containing a powerful spring that threw a hollow-charge projectile
P/O	Pilot Officer
OC	Officer Commanding
OP	Observation Post
RA	Royal Artillery
RAF	Royal Air Force
RAMC	Royal Army Medical Corps
RASC	Royal Army Service Corps
RE	Royal Engineers
Regiment	(British and Indian Army) originally of horse, dragoons or foot, raised by command of monarch, and later Parliament, and named after its colonel, originally a royal appointee. The regiment became the basic organisation of the British Army and Indian Army, for armour, artillery, engineers, signals, and logistic units' equivalent to battalions of those arms in other armies. In the case of the infantry, the British or Indian Army battalion belongs to a regiment, of which there may be one or more battalions and who may not serve together in the same area, or even in the same theatre of operations.
Regt	Regiment
RHA	Royal Horse Artillery

RN	Royal Navy
RSM	Regimental Sergeant Major
Sapper	The equivalent of private in the Royal Engineers, often used as a term for all engineers
SEAC	South East Asia Command
SR	Special Reserve
Staff Sergeant	The senior sergeant of a non-infantry company (cf. colour sergeant)
Vickers	Slang for a specific-named medium machine-gun belt-fed, water-cooled with a firing rate of 500 rounds per minute. Last fired in action by the British Army in 1962.
Wadi	Arabic for valley
WRNS	Women's Royal Naval Service

Bibliography

Over the years since 1855 many books have been published about the Victoria Cross and about individual winners of the award. Listed here are some of those books together with general histories which deal with the background to the campaigns and battles of the First and Second World War in which these gallantry awards were won.

However, three books deserve special mention: Chaz Bowyer, *For Valour: The Air VCs* (London: Kimber, 1978; Grub Street, 1992); John Winton, *The Victoria Cross at Sea* (London: Michael Joseph, 1978); Nora Buzzell, *The Register of the Victoria Cross* (Cheltenham: compiled for the quarterly magazine *This England*, 1981 and 1988).

Bowyer's book, which covers all air VCs from 1914, is the result of exemplary and painstaking research. Delving beyond the citations, Bowyer interviewed VC winners themselves, their comrades, friends and families. In this way he was able to prove, for instance, that Flight Sergeant Arthur Aaron was not shot down and killed by an enemy fighter but by the gunner of another British aircraft. For this revelation he was vilified by the head of the Air Historical Branch, who considered that citations were sacrosanct. He was mistaken; it is a historian's responsibility to find out and tell the truth, and this Bowyer does in *The Air VCs*.

Winton does a similar service for the Navy, by describing in detail the sea actions in which Victoria Crosses were won.

The *Register of the Victoria Cross* presents a condensed version of every VC citation published between 1855 and 1982, the then most recent date of a VC award. Also, it contains a small photograph of virtually every Victoria Cross winner. For VC holders after this date there are now a number of excellent works, many coming after the interest aroused by the 150th anniversary of the instigation of the Victoria Cross.

Books

Arthur, Max, *Forgotten Voices of the Great War*, Imperial War Museum, 2002.

Arthur, Max, *Symbol of Courage*, Sidgwick & Jackson, 2004.

Ashcroft, Michael, *Victoria Cross Heroes*, Headline Books, 2006; pbk 2007.

Bailey, Roderick (in association with the Imperial War Museum), *Forgotten Voices: Victoria Cross,* Ebury Press, 2011.

Bancroft, James W, *The Victoria Cross Roll of Honour*, Aim High Productions, 1989.

Bancroft, James W, *Deeds of Valour: A Victorian Military and Naval History Trilogy*, House of Heroes, 1994.

Bancroft, James W, *Local Heroes: Boer War VCs*, House of Heroes, 2003.

Bancroft, James W, *Zulu War Heroes: The Defence of Rorke's Drift*, James W Bancroft, 2004.

Batchelor, Peter F, and Matson, Christopher, *VCs of the First World War: The Western Front 1915*, Wrens Park Publishing, 1999.

Bond, Brian (ed.), *Victorian Military Campaigns*, Hutchinson, 1967.

Braddon, Russell, *Cheshire VC*, Evans Brothers, 1954.

Cooksley, Peter G, *VCs of the First World War: The Air VCs*, Wrens Park Publishing, 1999.

Cowper, Marcus, *The Words of War: British Forces' Personal Letters and Diaries during WW2*, Mainstream Publishing/Imperial War Museum, 2010.

Crawthorne, Nigel, *The True Story behind every VC Winner since WW2*, John Blake, 2007.

Creagh, E M O'Moore and Humphris, E (eds), *The V.C. and D.S.O. Book: The Victoria Cross 1856–1920*, Naval & Military Press, Standard Art Book Co., 1924.

Crook, M J, *The Evolution of the Victorian Cross*, Midas Books, 1975.

Doherty, Richard, and Truesdale, David, *Irish Winners of the Victoria Cross*, Four Courts Press, 2000.

Farwell, Byron, *Queen Victoria's Little Wars*, Allen Lane, 1973; reprint, Wordsworth, 1999.

Featherstone, Donald, *Victoria's Enemies: A–Z of British Colonial Warfare*, Blandford, 1989.

Feilding, Rowland, *War Letters to a Wife*, Medici Society, 1929.

Fraser, George MacDonald, *Quartered Safe Out Here: A Recollection of the War in Burma*, HarperCollins, 1992.

Fraser, Ian, *Frogman VC*, Angus & Robertson, 1957.

Giddings, Robert, *Imperial Echoes: Eye-Witness Accounts of Victoria's Little Wars*, Leo Cooper, 1996.

Gilbert, Martin, *The Second World War*, Weidenfeld & Nicolson, 1989.

Glanfield, John, *Bravest of the Brave: The Story of the Victoria Cross*, Sutton Publishing, 2005.

Gliddon, Gerald, *VCs of the First World War: 1914*, Budding Books, 1997.

Gliddon, Gerald, *VCs of the First World War: Spring Offensive 1918*, Sutton Publishing, 1997.

Gliddon, Gerald, *VCs of the First World War: The Somme*, Budding Books, 1997.

Gliddon, Gerald, *VCs of the First World War: Arras and Messines 1917*, Wrens Park Publishing, 2000.

Gliddon, Gerald, *VCs of the First World War: The Final Days 1918*, Sutton Publishing, 2000.

Gliddon, Gerald, *VCs of the First World War: The Road to Victory 1918*, Sutton Publishing, 2000.

Gordon, Lawrence, and Joslin, Edward (eds), *British Battles and Medals*, Spink & Son, 1971.

Gurney, Gene, *The War in the Air*, Bonanza, 1962.

Harris, Barry, *Black Country VCs*, Black Country Society, 1985.

Harris, C, and Whippy, J, *The Greater Game: Sporting Icons Who Fell in the Great War*, Pen & Sword, 2000.

Hart, Sydney, *Submarine Upholder (Wanklyn VC)*, Melrose, 1966.

Harvey, David, *Monuments to Courage: Victoria Cross Head Stones and Memorials*, vols 1 and 2, Kevin & Kay Patience; reprint, Naval & Military Press, 1999.

Hastings, Macdonald, *More Men of Glory*, Hulton Press, 1959.

Haydon, A L, *The Book of the VC*, Andrew Melrose, 1906.

Haythornthwaite, Philip J, *The Colonial Wars Source Book*, Arms and Armour Press, 1997.

HMSO, *Victoria Cross Centenary Exhibition 1856–1956*, HMSO, 1956.

Holmes, Richard, *The First World War in Photographs*, Carlton Books/IWM, 2006.

Jameson, William S, *Submariners VC*, Peter Davies, 1962.

Keegan, John, *The Second World War*, Hutchinson, 1989.

Kirby, H L, and Walsh, R R, *Seven VCs of Stonyhurst College*, THCL Books, 1987.

Kitson, J A, *Story of the 4th Battalion 2nd King Edward VII's Own Ghurkha Rifles*, Gale & Polden, 1949.

Laffin, John, *British VCs of World War 2: A Study in Heroism*, Budding Books, 2000.

Lassen, Suzanne, *Anders Lassen VC: Story of a Courageous Dane*, Muller, 1965.

Liddle, Peter, *D-Day by Those Who were There*, Pen & Sword Books, 2004.

Macdonald, W James, *A Bibliography of the Victoria Cross*, privately published by author, Beddeck, Nova Scotia, 1995.

Macmillan, Norman, *The Royal Air Force in the Second World War*, vol. 2, 1940–1941, Harrap, 1944.

Magor, R B, *African General Service Medals*, R B Magor, 1979; reprint, Naval & Military Press, 1993.

Massie, Alastair, *The National Army Museum Book of the Crimean War: The Untold Stories*, Sidgwick & Jackson, 2004.

Masters, John, *The Road Past Mandalay*, Michael Joseph, 1961.

Ministry of Information, *Victoria Cross: Stories of VC Awards during the Second World War up to June 1943*, Ministry of Information, 1943.

Morgan, M, *D-Day Hero: CSM Stanley Hollis VC*, Sutton Publishing, 2004.

Mulholland, John, and Jordan, Alan (eds), *Victoria Cross Bibliography*, Victoria Cross Research Group, Spink & Son, 1999.

Owen, Frank, *The Campaign in Burma*, HMSO Official Report, 1946.

Pakenham, Thomas, *The Boer War*, Weidenfeld & Nicolson, and Avon Books, 1979.

Pakenham, Thomas, *The Scramble for Africa*, Weidenfeld & Nicolson, 1991; Abacus, 2002.

Parrish, Thomas (ed.), *The Simon and Schuster Encyclopaedia of World War 2*, Simon & Schuster, 1978.

Pemberton, W Baring, *Battles of the Boer War*, Batsford, 1964; Pan Books, 1969.

Phillips, C E Lucas, *Victoria Cross Battles of the Second World War*, Heinemann, 1973.

Ralph, Wayne, *Barker VC: The Life, Death and Legend of Canada's Most Decorated War Hero*, Grub Street, 1997.

Richards, D S, *The Savage Frontier: A History of the Anglo-Afghan Wars*, Macmillan, 1990; Pan Books, 2003.

Roe, F Gordon, *The Bronze Cross: Tribute to Those Who Won the Supreme Award for Valour in the Years 1940–45*, P R Gawthorn, 1945.

Sandford, Kenneth, *Mark of the Lion: The Story of Capt. Charles Upham, VC and Bar*, Hutchinson, 1962.

Scott, Kenneth Hare, *For Valour*, Garnett, 1949.

Sims, Edward H, *The Fighter Pilots*, Cassell, 1967.

Smyth, John, *The Story of the Victoria Cross 1856–1963*, Muller, 1963.

Snelling, Stephen, *VCs of the First World War: Passchendaele 1917*, Sutton Publishing, 1998.

Snelling, Stephen, *VCs of the First World War: Gallipoli*, Wrens Park Publishing, 1999.

Sowards, Stuart E, *A Formidable Hero: R. H. Gray VC*, Canav Books, 1987.

Stevens, G R, *History of the 2nd King Edward VII's Own Goorkha Rifles*, vol. 3, Gale & Polden, 1952.

Thompson, Julian, *Forgotten Voices of Burma*, Ebury Press/Imperial War Museum, 2009.

Turner, John Frayn, *VCs of the Army, 1939–1951*, Harrap, 1956.

Turner, John Frayn, *VCs of the Royal Navy*, Harrap, 1956.

Turner, John Frayn, *VCs of the Air*, Harrap, 1960.
Whitman, J E A, *Gallant Deeds of the War*, OUP, 1941.
Whitworth, Alan, *Yorkshire VCs*, Pen & Sword, 2007.

Journals & Magazines

Frost, Richard (ed.) (2001) *Journal of the King's Royal Rifle Corps Association*
Best, Brian (ed.) (2004) *Journal of The Victoria Cross Society*, Editions 1-4
The Regiment of Fusiliers (1999) English Life Publications
The Register of the Victoria Cross (1988) This England Books
Turner, John Frayn (2001) *VCs of the Air*, Wrens Park Publishing

Websites

National Archives, www.nationalarchives.gov.uk/documentsonline
National Archives Library, www.library.nationalarchives.gov.uk/library
London Gazette newspaper, www.gazette-online.co.uk
Oxford Dictionary of Biography, www.oxforddnb.com
Grave sites, www.findagrave.com
Imperial War Museum, www.iwm.org
Ministry of Defence Records, www.mod.uk/defencenews
Rorke's Drift, www.rorkesdrift.com
Green Howards Regiment, www.greenhowards.org.uk
Australian VC holders, www.diggerhistory.info
Victoria Cross, www.victoriacross.org.uk
Victoria Cross Society, www.victoriacrosssociety.com

Note: mention of a website does not guarantee that by the time of publication it will be in existence, therefore the author and publisher cannot be held responsible for any omissions or changes.